RICHARD PAYNE KNIGHT
EXPEDITION INTO SICILY

Charles Gore: *Ruins of the Temple of Jupiter at Agrigentum*, 1777. Pen and brown ink with brown and grey wash over pencil, 26.5 × 43.2 cm (Oo.4-24).

RICHARD PAYNE KNIGHT
EXPEDITION INTO SICILY

Edited by Claudia Stumpf

British Museum Publications

Introduction and Notes © 1986 Claudia Stumpf

Richard Payne Knight: Expedition into Sicily.
1777 © Goethe- und Schiller-Archiv, Weimar

Published by British Museum Publications Ltd
46 Bloomsbury Street, London WC1B 3QQ

British Library Cataloguing in Publication Data
Knight, Richard Payne
   Expedition into Sicily.
   1. Sicily—Description and travel—
   To 1900
   I. Title II. Stumpf, Claudia
   914.5'8047   DG863
ISBN 0-7141-1627-0

Designed by James Shurmer

Set in Monotype Lasercomp Bembo
and printed in Great Britain by
BAS Printers Limited, Over Wallop,
Hampshire

The publishers are grateful to the present owner
of Downton Castle for the generous donation
which made the publication of this book
possible

To Zecki

Contents

Preface	*page* 7
Introduction	9
Bibliographical Note	20
Notes on the Introduction	20
Expedition into Sicily. 1777	23
Notes on the 'Expedition into Sicily'	67

One of Charles Gore's Sicilian watercolours (Weimar, Goethe Nationalmuseum).

Photographic Acknowledgements Illustrations are from the British Museum, unless otherwise acknowledged in the captions. The publishers are grateful to all those who have given their permission to reproduce works in their collections, and also to the following for providing photographs: Courtauld Institute of Art, figs 1 and 3; Artothek, Planegg, Germany, fig. 6; Royal Academy of Arts, fig. 7.

Preface

When I undertook the somewhat hazardous journey to Weimar in 1980, I did not expect to make any 'art-historical discoveries'. The deadline for my MA report at the Courtauld Institute was only four weeks away and I was in rather a hurry to check some drawings by Charles Gore, an eighteenth-century English amateur artist, at the Goethe-Nationalmuseum in Weimar.

Gore had made an 'Expedition into Sicily' in 1777, with the German painter Jakob Philipp Hackert and the young English dilettante Richard Payne Knight. While Hackert and Gore had recorded the stations of their journey in a series of drawings and watercolours, Knight had written a diary. This journal had been translated and published by Johann Wolfgang von Goethe more than thirty years after the 'Expedition', but the original English version of the text was generally thought to be lost. The aim of my report was to establish the interrelation between the journal – in Goethe's translation – and a series of Sicilian views by Hackert and Gore kept in the Payne Knight Bequest at the British Museum.

Having completed my research at the Goethe-Nationalmuseum, I found myself with a day to spare in Weimar and decided to explore some of the less accessible sites. The Goethe- und Schiller-Archiv looked a challenging prospect, an imposing building perched on the side of a hill above the old town. I used my search for 'any material on Goethe and Knight' as an excuse for my curiosity rather than a serious scholarly suggestion, but was allowed to visit the catalogue room. The librarian's answer to my somewhat vague request took me completely by surprise: 'Yes, we do have material

Preface *continued*

on Knight: the English manuscript of a diary which was later translated by Goethe.' When I first turned the pages of the text, densely covered in an immaculate calligraphic hand, I felt as if I had found a long-lost score by Beethoven or a poem by Goethe himself.

There was, of course, no call for this kind of enthusiasm. Knight's diary may be an entertaining piece of eighteenth-century travel literature, but it is not a masterpiece by any means. Its points of interest, as well as its shortcomings, are discussed and annotated below. The text is reproduced as closely to the original manuscript as possible, including inconsistencies in spelling and nomenclature. However, paragraphs have been introduced to make for greater readability.

That Knight's 'Expedition into Sicily' is finally published in full and in its original English version is largely due to the patience and generosity of the present owner of Downton Castle and Professor Dr K.-H. Hahn, Director of the Goethe- und Schiller-Archiv, Weimar. I would also like to thank the Mellon Foundation and the Central Research Fund, University of London, for travel grants to Weimar, Shropshire and Rome; the staff of the Department of Prints and Drawings, British Museum, the Goethe-Nationalmuseum and the Goethe- und Schiller-Archiv for their efficiency and tolerance; Giulia Bartrum, Ian Chilvers, Celia Clear, Teresa Francis, Professor Michael Kitson, Dr Nicholas Penny, Dr Alex Potts, Andrew Prescott, Lindsay Stainton, Diana Uhlman and my parents for scholarly advice and editorial help, and my husband, Graham Brigg, for his indestructible sense of humour.

Introduction

Richard Payne Knight (1751–1824) was 26 years old when he travelled to Sicily in 1777. A portrait painted a few years earlier by Nathaniel Hone (fig. 1) shows a sensitive and rather meek young man, though his glance betrays inquisitiveness and the right hand placed symbolically on the spine of a book seems to confirm this notion. The young Knight was an insatiable reader, and although – owing to his poor health – he never went to university and his education was begun at a comparatively late age, he was soon steeped in the Classics, became an excellent scholar of Greek and developed a keen interest in the arts and history of the ancients.

Another portrait, painted about twenty years later by Sir Thomas Lawrence (fig. 2), records the somewhat ambiguous changes the youth had undergone. He is represented as the established scholar he became, the renowned collector and critic, trustee and benefactor of the British Museum and one of the country's most influential connoisseurs. The book, in the earlier portrait held discreetly at his side, is now interposed between the man of learning and the spectator, who is relegated to a deferentially low viewpoint. Knight's disdainful glance is directed towards 'loftier heights' than before. The gestures of his hands – one pointing didactically at an illustration, the other confidently holding the folio in his lap – match the superior ex-

1 Nathaniel Hone (1718–84): *Richard Payne Knight*, about 1775. Oil on canvas, 66 × 55 cm (Mr D. P. H. Lennox).

pression on his face: the timid youth has matured into a truly 'Arrogant Connoisseur'.[1]

Knight came from a family of *nouveau-riche* Shropshire ironmasters, whose fortune he had inherited. This enabled him to lead the life of a gentleman and scholar. He travelled, designed and built his own houses and gardens, collected works of art and published articles and books on a wide range of topics. His interests were varied, and although he seems to have tried to emulate the ideas and ideals of traditional scholarship and learning, he became better known for his spectacular *faux-pas*: the first a publication on the 'worship of Priapus' – the survival of pagan phallic cults in a Roman Catholic festival in southern Italy – in 1786;[2] the second his unfavourable assessment of the Elgin Marbles, discussed below. Despite his controversial opinions in these matters, he was widely recognised as a scholar and arbiter of taste by his contemporaries. He had undertaken the obligatory Grand Tour in 1772–3 (and was again in Italy in 1776–8), decided to build for himself a new house at Downton in 1772, was returned as Member of Parliament for Leominster in 1780, was elected a member of the Society of Dilettanti in 1781 and appointed a Trustee of the British Museum in 1814. He had published his *Analytical Essay on the Greek Alphabet* in 1791, a 'didactic poem' – *The Landscape* – in 1794, another poem, *The Progress of Civil Society*, in 1796 and, probably his greatest success, the *Analytical Inquiry into the Principles of Taste* in 1805. His major works on the arts were the *Specimens of Antient Sculpture* of 1809 and, in 1818, his *Inquiry into the Symbolical Language of Ancient Art and Mythology*.[3]

As seems to be suggested by Lawrence's portrait, Knight saw himself – with some justification – as the country's foremost connoisseur. At the time of the expedition to Sicily, however, he

2 Sir Thomas Lawrence (1769–1830): *Richard Payne Knight*, about 1794. Oil on canvas, 127 × 102 cm (Manchester University, Whitworth Art Gallery).

3 Thomas Hearne: *View of Downton Castle*, 1785. Watercolour over pencil, 34 × 48·5 cm (Mr D. P. H. Lennox).

had by no means acquired his later arrogance. He was young and inexperienced and, as will become evident from the far-fetched references and often pompous tone of the diary, seems to have felt the need to establish himself as a gentleman-scholar. It is very likely that he was trying to emulate the style of the Society of Dilettanti, a group of high-living young aristocrats who were setting new standards in scholarly publication by sponsoring the archaeological investigation of Classical sites in both Italy and Greece.[4]

It was in the wake of this movement that the remains of Greek civilisation in southern Italy were to become famous in the following decades. Sicily held a particular fascination for the eighteenth-century traveller. 'Our earliest education has made us acquainted with those classic regions; Poetry and History have rendered their topography familiar to us', wrote Henry Swinburne in 1776.[5] To Knight and his contemporaries the island, the ancient Trinacria, was the scene 'where so many mighty Cities have flourished in Art and Arms, where so many numerous fleets and Armies have fought for Universal Empire'.[6] Here Ulysses had outwitted the Cyclops, Aeneas had rested on his flight from Troy, the Greek tyrants of Syracuse and Acragas had vied with Athens herself in pomp and splendour. Here Carthage and Rome had fought for supremacy in the ancient world, the Slave Wars had paved the way for Spartacus, Verres had committed his wilful crimes and Sextus Pompey used the 'granary of Rome' as a stronghold in his fight against Octavian. To travel in Sicily was a journey into the past, a 'Golden Age' which every educated man had been taught to revere and a world 'in which the only foreigners are those who are foreigners also to letters and all useful and agreeable knowledge.'[7]

Knight and his travelling companions were well aware of these associations at the outset of their journey. It is likely, in fact, that they were hoping for more tangible results from their expedition than a mere search for the original setting of important episodes in Classical history or Greek pastoral poetry. Since the rediscovery of the Doric temples at Paestum in the 1740s,[8] Doric architecture had become a major topic of scholarly investigation and the most famous temples built in this style outside Greece were known to have existed in Sicily. Descriptions of their remains had appeared at regular intervals since the sixteenth century,[9] despite the alleged hazards of robbers and the dreaded eruptions of Mount Etna. The most recent scholarly accounts had been published in 1771 by the Baron von Riedesel[10] and in 1773 by Patrick Brydone.[11] Neither of these accounts was illustrated, however, and this is where Knight and his companions may have seen their chance for scholarly distinction as well as a possible financial reward. To produce a carefully illustrated and well-written guide to the remains of Greek civilisation in Sicily seems to have been the ultimate goal of the expedition.

Knight had left England in 1776, accompanied by the young watercolour painter John Robert Cozens (1752–97), with the help of whose sketches we can follow their route via Switzerland to Italy.[12] They arrived in Rome in the autumn of that same year and Knight must have begun his preparations for the Sicilian venture almost immediately. We do not know whether he was already acquainted with his travelling companions, the fashionable German landscape painter Jakob Philipp Hackert and his amateur pupil, the wealthy Charles Gore, before he came to Italy. They may have met in the intellectually bustling climate of the Roman salons in the autumn of 1776 and decided to go to Sicily together out of a shared passion for travelling and topographical representation, as well as an interest in contemporary archaeological investigation. It is more likely, however, that the trip was planned well in advance, especially since Knight had already been in Italy in 1772–3 and would certainly have had the opportunity of meeting the German painter.

Hackert (1737–1807)[13] had made his way from Berlin via Paris to Rome, where he had settled in 1768. He had established himself with characteristic efficiency and his mass-produced, decorative views of topographical subjects and made-to-measure depictions of natural phenomena soon made him extremely popular with fashionable Roman society. His reputation as a drawing-master was no less widespread. He was a teacher to English gentlemen-travellers, like Charles Gore, as well as to Neapolitan princesses and intellectual celebrities like Goethe.

Charles Gore (1729–1807)[14] was probably the most amiable of the three travelling companions. A Yorkshire merchant, shipbuilder and collector, he had come to Italy with his family in 1774. His youngest daughter had married an English gentleman living in Florence, and Gore, whose circumstances allowed him to spend his time as he pleased, had rented a house in Rome and begun to take drawing lessons. He and Hackert had spent several summers sketching and exploring the picturesque surroundings of the city together, and had become close friends.

The expedition to Sicily, so Knight tells us in his diary, began on 12 April 1777, when the party left Naples by boat. Their first port of call was Paestum, an obvious stopping place, with its Doric temples similar to those of Sicily. From there they sailed westwards to Milazzo, on the north coast of Sicily, passing the Lipari Islands on the way. Having disembarked, they made their way along the north coast to Palermo, where they stayed for several days. Then the companions concentrated on the main business of their journey, recording and measuring the Greek

4 *Jakob Philipp Hackert*. Engraving by E. Morace after Augusto Nicodemo (Kunstsammlungen Veste Coburg).

5 Johann Joseph Zoffany (1733–1810):
George, 3rd Earl Cowper, with the Family of Charles Gore, about 1775.
Oil on canvas, 78 × 97.5 cm (Yale Center for British Art, Paul Mellon Collection).
Gore is playing the violincello, accompanied by his daughter Emily on the square piano.
In the middle of the group is George, 3rd Earl Cowper, and behind the piano is his wife, Hannah Anne, Gore's youngest daughter.
Mrs Gore is on the right with her third daughter.

temples at Segesta, Selinunte, Agrigento and Syracuse, and after an adventurous climb to the crater of Mount Etna they left the island from the port of Catania, three months after they had set out from Naples. They returned to Rome in July 1777.

There they began to work up the material they had collected on the journey. Hackert and Gore produced 'finished' versions of the sketches they had made in Sicily. J. R. Cozens, who had concentrated on his own work during Knight's absence, was employed to provide interpretations of some of the more romantic scenes, for instance the hauntingly beautiful illustration of the travellers' moonlit encampment on the slopes of Mount Etna (Pl. 14). Knight, who presumably supervised all these activities, seems already to have decided on the basic contents of his planned publication, since out of the hundreds of sketches produced by the artists he took only twenty-four back to England.[15] Their subjects are closely related to the major themes of the text. While the written account of the journey would have provided the basis for the selection of illustrations, it is unlikely that it was composed in its present form during this period. For historical details and references to Classical literature, Knight would have had to consult his library, as he confirms in a letter to the painter George Romney, written on 24 November 1776: '. . . you will excuse inaccuracies and remember, that I write as a traveller without books and memorandums'.[16] It must have been after his return to England that Knight wrote the final version of his account and probably also added the concluding part on Sicilian affairs in general. He was still engaged on the project in 1782 – five years after the expedition – when he passed Hackert's and Gore's watercolours on to Thomas Hearne (1744–1817), a well-known topographical artist, to put them into final shape for publication. Hearne's contribution seems to be apparent in the simplification of motifs, the introduction of picturesque foreground detail and subdued, almost monochrome colouring, reminiscent of his preparatory watercolours for the engravings in the *Antiquities of Great Britain*.[17]

Knight, however, never saw the project through to conclusion. There is, in fact, no further record of the diary until its publication by Goethe more than thirty years later. Goethe seems to have found the text amongst Hackert's papers, some of which he published after the artist's death.[18]

But why did Knight abandon the project after putting so much effort into it? It seems unlikely that such carefully prepared material was meant for private circulation only. The best explanation is perhaps the publication of rival accounts of Sicily; in particular, in 1781 – the very time when Knight may have been preparing for publication – the Abbé de Saint-Non's lavishly illustrated folios on southern Italy began to appear.[19] They incorporated the one feature which might have made Knight's book new and interesting: the juxtaposition of text and illustrations.

Another important book, a travel guide to all the antiquities of Sicily written by the internationally renowned Sicilian scholar and collector Prince Ignazio di Biscari, appeared in 1781,[20] and an impressively illustrated work by J. Houel, *Voyage pittoresque des Isles de Sicile, de Malte et de Lipari*, between 1784 and 1787.[21] There seems almost to have been a rush to explore and publish the antiquities of Sicily in the 1780s and it would not be surprising if Knight had abandoned his project in view of such competition.

As was said earlier, Knight may have planned a scholarly account of Greek architecture in Sicily in the vein of the pioneering publications of the Society of Dilettanti, possibly even as a kind of warrant for his membership there. If so, he was certainly

6 Johann Heinrich Wilhelm Tischbein (1751–1829): *Portrait of Goethe in the Roman Campagna*, 1786/7. Oil on canvas, 164 × 206 cm (Frankfurt, Städelsches Kunstinstitut).

outclassed by Saint-Non and Biscari even before he had published. His failure to present the Sicilian project to the public may have been more beneficial to his career as a scholar, however, than its publication would have been. The superficial references to the Classics and the rather obvious conclusions Knight presents in the diary would hardly have met the highly scientific standards and exacting methods of the Dilettanti.

The complete English version of Knight's journal is here published for the first time. It is divided into two sections, one a narrative of the journey, the second more general in outlook. The first part contains 'many interesting descriptions and important observations on moral, administrative and other matters', as Goethe put it.[22] It is written in straightforward diary form, with place-names and dates in the margin indicating the various stages of the journey (fig. 10). (They have been inserted in the body of the text in the present edition.) Most of the places visited by the three travelling companions were Greek sites, such as Paestum, Segesta and Selinunte, which were obviously the main focus of the expedition. This emphasis is matched by the illustrations, most of which show architectural fragments, ruined temples or overall views of the sites. Knight gives detailed descriptions of these remains, and provides a diffuse account of their history. He mentions such episodes as the destruction of Himera, the ingenious cruelty of Phalaris, Segesta's role in the First Punic War, and so on, and expects his readers to fill in the

7 Sir Joshua Reynolds (1723–92): *Group Portrait of the Society of Dilettanti*, 1777–9. Oil on canvas, 198 × 150 cm (The Society of Dilettanti). One of two pictures painted to celebrate a meeting on 2 March 1777 at which Sir William Hamilton (pointing to one of the four volumes publishing his collection) was introduced as a member.

details of the story as a matter of course. This apparently intimate knowledge of the Classics is impressive, but on closer inspection Knight's information often turns out to be inaccurate. What appear to be erudite quotations from obscure sources are in fact references used by almost every eighteenth-century writer on Sicily or southern Italy. Concluding his passage on the temples of Paestum, for instance, Knight praises the region's dry and fertile soil, which, he says, is 'worthy of the *rosaria Paesti*, so celebrated by the Roman poets'.[23] The Latin phrase and reference to Roman poetry on a topic as obscure as the cultivation of roses in an early Greek colony in southern Italy baffle the modern reader. However, in Richard de Saint-Non's account, published in 1781, one finds exactly the same reference, not merely flung in the reader's face but carefully annotated and explained.[24] Saint-Non did not actually discover the quotation either. It was, in fact, a standard reference in eighteenth-century commentaries on Paestum.[25]

There is no need to dwell on Knight's scholarly inaccuracies, which are indicated and explained wherever possible in the notes. Thorough research and originality of concept were comparatively new requirements for eighteenth-century writers, most of whom, like Knight, were still attached to more traditional methods: that is, the use of accepted Classical source material and standard references handed down over centuries. It must also be remembered that Knight was a novice in this field and may have adopted a deliberately arrogant style in an attempt to conceal his inexperience.

The first part of the diary also deals with natural phenomena, such as the volcanic Lipari Islands and Mount Etna. In fact, the tone of Knight's narration changes according to his subject and seems to become less pretentious and more interesting the further he digresses from archaeological investigation. At the summit of Mount Etna his antiquarian pretensions crumble before the view:

The whole Island of Sicily, Malta, Calabria, & the Liparis appear just under one as in a map. The parts were all obscured in the blue tint of the morning and the whole together seemed wrapt in silence and repose. I felt myself elevated above humanity, & looked down with Contempt upon the mighty objects of Ambition under me. The Scenes where so many mighty Cities have flourished in Art and Arms, where so many numerous fleets and Armies have fought for Universal Empire, seemed no more than a Spot . . .[26]

Probably the most entertaining passages of the diary are Knight's observations on local scenery and customs; for instance, his disappointment at finding the 'nymphs' at the fountain of Arethusa in Syracuse nothing like Virgil's description of them, but 'no other than a company of the most dirty old washerwomen, I ever beheld'.[27] Or his annoyance at the magistrate of Patti who not only 'dignified himself with the title of Governor' but in this function arrested Knight and his party for spying when they attempted to draw an old watch-tower by the sea.[28]

The journal ends with the inevitable quote from the *Aeneid*, followed by Knight's enquiry into the general affairs of Sicily. What he found most remarkable was the discrepancy between the wealth and political importance extolled in Classical literature and the contemporary desolation of the island. In an attempt to explain these changes, Knight tried to see the events in a general historical context, employing the theories of rise and decline so popular with historians of the period. The conclusion he arrived at is representative of the 'enlightened libertarianism' he shared with many young Whigs of his generation.[29] He puts the blame for political, economical and judicial grievances, for the corruption of taste and decline of culture, on the 'sour mythology of the Christians'[30] and their overwhelming influence in Sicily. It may well have been this blatant imposition of personal views on world history which prompted the equally dogmatic Goethe to omit this section of the text altogether.

Knight's journal is not a masterpiece – rather a young dilettante's showpiece of his Classical education. While many of his observations – and even errors – may seem amusing or quaint to us today, there can be little doubt that to his contemporaries they would have appeared 'behind the times' – an effort to keep up with contemporary scholarship rather than providing a new interpretation. In its rigid acceptance of traditional source material and arrogant self-assurance it may remind the reader of a better-known incident in Knight's life: his rejection of the Elgin Marbles. Called upon as the country's leading arbiter of taste, Knight gave his evidence concerning the value of the marbles before a Select Parliamentary Committee in 1816.[31] He held the opinion that the sculptures were not only badly damaged, but that they did not rank 'in the first class of art' and had been added to the Parthenon 'in the time of Hadrian'.[32] Since his was the only voice on the committee to disclaim the excellence of the marbles, Knight's 'performance' has always been considered 'a dismal one' which 'instantly and finally' destroyed 'his reputation as a connoisseur'.[33] What seems to have been overlooked by most of his critics is the fact that Knight could – and indeed did – refer to a scholarly tradition of long standing. The view that some of the Parthenon sculptures were Hadrianic was well established, and had been backed up with references from Classical source material by scholars since the seventeenth century.[34] It had been discussed in the eighteenth century by the Dilettanti Society's protégés Stuart and Revett in their acclaimed work on Athenian architecture,[35] and had recently been reiterated in a lecture given by the leading European antiquarian E. Q. Visconti, which had been translated and, in fact, published with the Elgin Committee report![36] These arguments, however, would not convince a new generation of artists and critics whose judgment was based on their own observation and knowledge rather than that of others.

Where Knight may have failed concerning both the 'Sicilian Project' and the assessment of the Elgin Marbles was not in his scholarship or taste, but in too uncritical an acceptance of second-hand references, his rigid adherence to traditional values and personal affiliations which may, at times, have obstructed a wider outlook.

As a 'man of taste' Knight had certain responsibilities, not just concerning the arts but in social and moral matters too. His attitudes were determined by his education, which was based on the revered model of the ancients. If he travelled it was not for adventure but to broaden his horizons and recapture the spirit of the Classics, and if he looked at the Elgin Marbles, this had less to do with pleasure or the enjoyment of art than an assessment of their value as 'fragments' of history or education for the artists of his time. His scholarship – of which the Sicilian journal is a typical example – was based on 'knowing' rather than 'seeing', learned references and tradition rather than originality and innovation. Other comparable journals – notably Goethe's *Italienische Reise* – are undoubtedly of greater literary value and sensitivity. Nevertheless, Knight's diary is of interest because it provides a classic example of the outlook and preoccupations of an educated eighteenth-century gentleman-traveller and collector.

Bibliographical Note

In the Notes on the Introduction and on the 'Expedition into Sicily', frequent reference is made to the following:

Arrogant Connoisseur: M. Clarke and N. Penny (eds), *The Arrogant Connoisseur: Richard Payne Knight 1751–1824*, exhibition catalogue, Whitworth Art Gallery (Manchester 1982), with full bibliography.

Sales Catalogue: a *Catalogue of a select portion of the Library of John Crosse, Esq. and a portion of the Library of the late Richard Payne Knight, Esq.* sold by 'Mr. Evans, at his house, No. 93, Pall-Mall' on 21 December 1829. The catalogue does not distinguish between books from the libraries of Crosse and Knight, but most of the more obscure works on Sicily must surely have belonged to Knight.

Classical texts

Cicero, *The Verrine Orations*, ed. Loeb (2 vols, London/New York 1928–35).

Diodorus Siculus, *History*, ed. Loeb (12 vols, London/New York and Cambridge, Mass. 1933–67).

Strabo, *Geography*, ed. Loeb (8 vols, London/New York, 1917–32).

Virgil, *Eclogues, Georgics, Aeneid I–VI*, ed. Loeb (London/New York, rev. ed. 1935).

Notes on the Introduction

1 For the most recent account of Knight's life and work, see *Arrogant Connoisseur*.

2 Ibid., 50–64.

3 Knight's activities and publications are discussed with full bibliography in *Arrogant Connoisseur*.

4 The most comprehensive account of the Society's activities is still Lionel Cust, *History of the Society of Dilettanti* (London 1914).

5 H. Swinburne, *Travels in the Two Sicilies* (London 1783), I, XVI.

6 See p. 56 below. For eighteenth-century attitudes to Sicily, see H. Tuzet, *La Sicile au XVIIIe siècle vue par les voyageurs étrangers* (Strasbourg 1955), and A. Momigliano, 'The Rediscovery of Greek History in the Eighteenth Century: The Case of Sicily', in *Studies in Eighteenth-Century Culture*, IX (1979), with literature.

7 Pierre Jean Grosley, *Observations sur l'Italie et sur les Italiens données en 1764, sous le nom de deux gentilhommes suédois* (London 1770), II, 254, quoted in F. Haskell and N. Penny, *Taste and the Antique* (London/New Haven 1981), 45.

8 See S. Lang, 'The Early Publications of the Temples at Paestum', *Journal of the Warburg and Courtauld Institutes*, XIII (London 1950), 48–64.

9 For an account of publications on Sicilian history and affairs from the Renaissance to the early nineteenth century, see A. Momigliano, 'La riscoperta della Sicilia antica da T. Fazello a P. Orsi', *Studi Urbinati di Storia, Filosofia e Letteratura*, Lettere Italiane (1978), Nuova Serie B, no. 1–2.

10 The first German edition of Riedesel's account appeared anonymously under the title *Reise durch Sicilien und Grossgriechenland* (Zurich 1771). The first English translation was published in 1773. (Knight must have known one of these, see p. 77, n. 116.) Riedesel was a close friend of J. J. Winckelmann, to whom this description of Sicilian antiquities in a series of letters was dedicated. The latest edition is by G. Richter (Berlin 1965).

11 P. Brydone, *A Tour through Sicily and Malta*, in a series of letters to William Beckford (London 1773), 2 vols. A copy of the 1776 edition is in the *Sales Catalogue*, lot 671.

12 See *Arrogant Connoisseur*, cat. nos 129–32.

13 Hackert's life and work are discussed in B. Lohse, *Jakob Philipp Hackert, Leben und Anfänge seiner Kunst* (Emsdetten 1936), and more recently by W. Krönig, 'Jakob Philipp Hackert. Ein Werk- und Lebensbild', in *Heroismus und Idylle – Landschaft um 1800*, exhibition catalogue, Wallraf-Richartz-Museum (Cologne 1984).

W. Krönig has also published an article on Hackert's Sicilian views: 'Philipp Hackerts Ansichten griechischer Tempel in Sizilien (1777)', supplement to exhibition catalogue *Berlin und die Antike* (Berlin 1979), and another study on the subject by the same author is due to appear in 1986.

14 A biography of Gore by Goethe (who used notes made by Gore's daughter Eliza) is published by E. Beutler, in *Johann Wolfgang Goethe. Gedenkausgabe der Werke, Briefe und Gespräche* (Zurich 1965), XIII, 598–608.

15 These – and copies made by Thomas Hearne and J. R. Cozens – are kept in the British Museum (Payne Knight Bequest Oo.4, nos 3–41). They are listed separately in a handwritten catalogue compiled by A. H. Smith (Department of Prints and Drawings: REG.A.60). One hundred and twelve sketches and watercolours of Sicilian views by Charles Gore are preserved in the Goethe-Nationalmuseum, Weimar (Th. Scr. 2. 2³ ff.).

16 J. Romney, *Memoirs of the Life and Works of George Romney* (London 1830), 332.

17 For Hearne and his artistic activities see *Arrogant Connoisseur*, cat. no. 114.

18 See Goethe, op. cit. (n. 14 above), 595.

19 Richard de Saint-Non, *Voyage Pittoresque ou description des Royaumes de Naples et de la Sicile* (Paris 1781–6).

20 Ignazio Paterno, Principe di Biscari, *Viaggio per tutte le antichità della Sicilia* (Naples 1781).

21 J. Houel, *Voyage pittoresque des Isles de Sicile, de Malte et de Lipari* (Paris 1784–7). The Goethe-Nationalmuseum, Weimar, preserves watercolours of Houel's Sicilian trip amongst Gore's papers.

22 Goethe, op. cit. (n. 14 above), 488.

23 See p. 29 below.

24 Richard de Saint-Non, op. cit. (n. 19 above), III, 153–62.

25 According to S. Lang, op. cit. (n. 8 above), passages on the twice-flowering roses at Paestum and their cultivation first appear in Giuseppe Antonini, Barone di San Biasca, *La Lucania; discorsi* (Naples 1745), III.

26 See p. 56 below.

27 See p. 48 below.

28 See p. 33 below.

29 The quotation is taken from *Arrogant Connoisseur*, 79. For an interesting exchange on Knight's political views, see the articles by N. Penny and A. Potts in *The Oxford Art Journal* V (1982), 1, 71–6.

30 See p. 66 below.

31 See House of Commons, Sessional Papers (1816), III. *Report from the Select Committee on the Earl of Elgin's Collection of Sculptured Marbles, etc.*, ordered by the House of Commons to be printed 25 March 1816, Reports Committee (I) 49–233.

32 Ibid., 40, 87.

33 William St Clair, *Lord Elgin and the Marbles* (Oxford 1983), 254, 258. See also A. H. Smith, 'Lord Elgin and his collection', in *Journal of Hellenic Studies* (1916), 338, who calls Knight's attitude 'plainly perverse'.

34 The most influential seventeenth-century publication to present this view was J. Spon and G. Wheler, *Voyage d'Italie, de Dalmatie, de Grèce et du Levant fait és années 1675 et 1676 par J. Spon . . . et G. Wheler* (Lyon 1678–80), in 3 vols. The plans and Classical sources (namely Pausanias) referred to as proof of the Hadrianic origin of the sculptures in this work as well as in de la Guilletière's *Athènes Ancienne & Nouvelle* (Paris 1675) are reiterated by E. G. Visconti, see n. 36 below.

35 J. Stuart and N. Revett, *The Antiquities of Athens measured and delineated by J.S. . . . and N.R.*, ed. W. Kinnard (London 1825), I, 65–82 (on Hadrianic architecture in Athens) and II, 24, note e (on the 'Hadrianic' sculptures of the Parthenon).

36 E. G. Visconti, *Memoir on the Sculptures which belonged to the Parthenon*, 'read at a Public Meeting of the 2 classes of the Royal Institute of France, 1815'. Published with the *Report from the Select Committee*, op. cit. (n. 31 above), 49–233.

Expedition into Sicily. 1777

8 Map of ancient Sicily, by G. de l'Isle, 1714 (British Library).

9 Map of Sicily, 1790 (British Library).

Expedition into Sicily. 1777

Left Rome April 3.
Naples.

April 12th 1777. we set out from Naples in a Felucca of twelve Oars, with an intention of making the turn of Sicily and visiting Paestum and the Lipari Islands in our way.

As soon as one is out of the Port of Naples, the most magnificent scene opens itself on every side. The city rising gradually from the shore, Mount Vesuvius smoking on one side, with Sorrento, Capri, Ischia, and Procida extending round to Cape Miseno in the form of an Amphitheatre, enriched with Palaces, Gardens, Woods and Ruins, are such an assemblage of objects, as are no where else to be seen. We enjoyed it in the utmost perfection, as the weather was extremely fine and the Spring in its bloom. The infinite variety of tints were all harmonized together by that pearly hue, which is peculiar to this delicious climate. (This Tint very particularly marks Claude Lorraine's Coloring.)[1] As we advanced into the open sea, the colours and forms seemed to sink into the Atmosphere and grow gradually indistinct, till at last the Sun withdrew its rays and left all in darkness.

During the night we slept in our Felucca, and before Sun-rise arrived at a little village, called Agropoli, five miles from Paestum. We immediately took horses and visited those venerable remains.

11 Charles Gore: *View of the Island of Procida*, 1777. Pen and black ink with watercolour over pencil, 21.4 × 43.8 cm. Inscribed in brown ink: 'Island of Procida near Naples' (1927-7-12-9).

10 (*left*) The opening lines of Knight's Sicilian diary (Weimar, Goethe- und Schiller-Archiv).

[Paestum, April 13th][2]

The first appearance of them is exceedingly striking – the three Temples, which are tolerably well preserved, rise one beyond the other in the midst of a rich and beautiful vale, surrounded by romantic Hills, covered with flowering Shrubs and Herbs. One of these is *Mons Albianus*, which is still covered with Ilexes, as mention'd by Virgil in his 3ᵈ Georgic:

Est lucos Silari circa *ilicibus*que virentem
Plurimus Alburnum volitans etc.[3]

It is now called Monte Vostiglione and is near the conflux of the Silarus and Tenager (now Selo and Negro). The Banks of the Silarus are still cover'd with thick woods, which during the Summer are much infested by the Astros or Asilus a kind of stinging fly, mention'd in the above Passage. The Tenager is an inconsiderable Stream, which sometimes dries in the summer-time; hence Virgil: sicci ripa.[4]

The Architecture of Paestum is the old Doric – the Columns, short and fluted, and near together, with broad flat Capitals and no bases. They are executed in a kind of porous petrifaction like that of the Lago *del Tartaro* near Tivoli. The Stones are exquisitely wrought and joined with the nicest exactitude, and like all the fine Works of the Ancients without Cement.[5] The colour is a whitish yellow, stained and corroded by the vicissitudes of weather, and overgrown with Moss and herbage; without being blackened by Smoke or intermixed with modern Buildings like the Ruins of Rome: hence the tints are extremely beautiful and picturesque.

When one examines the Parts near, they appear rude, massive and heavy; but seen at a proper distance, the general effect is grand, simple and even elegant. The rudeness appears then an artful negligence, and the heaviness a just and noble Stability.[6]

Besides the three Temples, there are the foundations of a small Amphitheatre, and considerable remains of the City Walls, within which the ground is all overspread with broken Columns and other fragments of ruined Edifices, which show the former magnificence of this ancient City. Among these one may trace the Ruins of a small Temple of a very singular kind. It stood between the great Temple or (as others suppose) the Basilica, and the Amphitheatre and appears to have been of the usual Doric form. The Columns are fluted in the Corinthian manner, with

12 Imaginary view of the temples at Paestum. Engraving after Jakob Philipp Hackert, 1789 (C. Stumpf).

interstices between the flutes, and the Capitals are of the same order, but very rude and simple. The entablature is Doric, but more charged with Members than that of the other buildings of Paestum. Between the Trigliffs are basso rilievos, the design of which appears to have been pure and elegant, but they are so corroded and mutilated in the small fragments which remain, that one cannot judge of the execution. Whether this Temple was built before the perfection of the Corinthian order, or after its decline, is uncertain. I am inclined to think the former for many reasons. The Corinthian order does not appear from any monuments extant, to have been perfected before the time of Augustus, nor to have declined till that of the Antonines.[7] As for the Story of its having been invented by an Architect of Corinth, from seeing an Acanthus, growing round a basket of flowers, it deserves little attention. Human Genius is always progressive in its operations, and in things of this kind generally slow. Men improve in works of taste more from observing the faults of others, than from any preconceiving Ideas of perfection.

The first rudiments of the Corinthian order are to be found among the Ruins of Thebes and Persepolis, and were brought into Europe probably about the time of Alexander the Great: but the Pride of the Greeks would never permit them, to acknowledge themselves Imitators in any thing. They claimed the invention and improvement of all arts, as owing to their own superior Genius, and not the effect of accident observation and experience.

The City of Paestum must have been in a state of decay long before the corruption, or even perfection of the Corinthian order,[8] as Strabo mentions its being deserted and unhealthy in his time,[9] and it is never spoken of as a place of any importance by the Historians of the Roman Wars in Italy.

The Buildings of the lower ages of Rome, when Architecture was corrupted,[10] are also in a different Stile from that abovemention'd. The Romans being Masters of the World, and having the rich quarries of Africa, Greece and Sicily, at their command, never imployed so much work upon so coarse a Material; But the Greek Republics being confined to a small space, were obliged to use whatever Material their own territory produced.

The exact time of the rise or fall of Paestum is not known, tho' both were probably very early. Its remains owe their preservation to the pestiferous quality of the Air, for had the place been habitable, they would have shared the fate of most of the works of the Greeks and Romans, and have been pulled in pieces, in order to imploy the materials in modern edifices. This poisonous air is produced by a salt stream, which flows from the mountains and stagnates under the Walls, where it petrifies and forms the kind of Stone of which the City was built. The petrifaction is extremely rapid, and some have supposed, that the Columns were cast in molds, as they consist of reeds, rushes etc. petrified by this Water; but I am inclined to think this opinion ill-founded.

The City was quadrangular, as appears by the Walls, which seem formerly to have been washed by the Sea, though now (owing to the petrifying stream) they are upwards of 500. yards distant from it. The new ground is very distinguishable from the old, being all nude petrifaction or Saltmarsh, whereas the old soil, within the Walls, and between them and the Mountains, is dry and fertile, worthy of the *rosaria Paesti*, so celebrated by the Roman Poets.

[Porto Palinuro, April 15th]

After spending a day among these noble remains of Grecian taste and Magnificence, we returned to our Felucca, and during the night coasted along to Cape Palinuro, which still retains the name of Aeneas's Pilot, who, according to Virgil, was killed here.[11] Finding the Wind contrary, we were obliged to go into a little Port of the same name, shelter'd from the South by the Promontory, and from the North and East by the mainland. The surrounding Country is extremely beautiful, the Vales being rich and fertile, and the Hills cloathed with Ilexes, Olives and flowering Shrubs, intermixed with Pastures. At a distance the vast Appenines appear white with Snow and form a noble termination to the Prospect.

We were detained in this little Port eight days by bad weather and the Cowardice of Neapolitan Seamen, and repented much of having left Paestum, where we could have passed our time so agreeably among the Ruins. However to imploy our time in something, we rambled about the Coast, having drawn our Felucca to shore, and made the best habitation we could, of it. A Cave in the Rock supplied us with a Kitchen, and, had it not been for our impatience to see Sicily, we could have passed our time agreeably enough *nunc veterum libris, nunc somno et inertibus horis.*[12]

In the course of our rambles about the Coast, we found a cavern of a very singular kind. It is formed in a sort of coarse Marble, intermixed with the same petrified gravel which appears in the other Parts of the Coast; but instead of seashells, this is full of human bones, broken into small pieces, and petrified into a solid Mass, with the Gravel, which lies between the beds of Marble in Strata of one, two or three feet thick. These Strata extend about sixty feet in length, and seemed to go far into the Mountain, which is of a considerable height.[13] I found a similar Rock at Nemezzo upon the Lake of Como, except that the bones formed a larger proportion, and instead of being between beds of Marble, were equally mixed thro' the whole Rock. The Island of Osero in the Adriatic, I have heard, is intirely composed of the same Material, which also appears in several Parts of Dalmatia. To offer any Conjectures, how these bones came here, would be useless, as the great revolutions, which this globe has evidently undergone, have their causes too remote for our Comprehension. We can only conclude, that Matter, endued with Motion, governed by the Laws of physical necessity, must, during the course of infinite time, have undergone every possible transmutation. In these infinite changes it must have been in disorder as well as order, which perhaps regularly spring from each other.

[Stromboli, April 23rd]

We left Porto Palinuro the 22nd. at 2. in the morning, but the weather being extremely calm, we did not reach Stromboli, till the morrow evening. About thirty miles before we arrived, Mount Aetna appeared white with Snow, and the smoke rolling down it. The lower regions of it, tho' far above the Horison, were for some time after invisible, owing to the density of the lower part of the Atmosphere. I was told, that it was frequently visible from the promontory of Palinurus, but during our stay there, the Air was never sufficiently clear.

The Island of Stromboli is a conical Mountain rising out of the Sea and intirely composed of Volcanic Matter.[14] The smoke issues at present from the Northwest side, near the summit, which is quite bare and composed of loose cinders. The other parts of it are richly cultivated and planted with Vines, the wine of which is much esteemed.

At night the fire from the Crater appeared, but very inconsiderable, owing to the fineness of the weather. During Rain or southerly Winds there is generally a small eruption. The noise is almost perpetual and very loud, resembling thunder. We intended to have gone up and examined the Crater, but were prevented by an ordinance of the King of Naples, which forbids any communication with the Inhabitants upon pain of performing quarantine. As this was a ceremony which we had no inclination to go thro' we set sail the same night for Lipari, and arrived there the morrow Morning.

[*Lipari, April 24th*]

The Town is situated at the bottom of a small Bay upon a Rock of Lava, projecting into the Sea, beautifully broken and hung with Shrubs. At a small distance it appears very elegant and pictoresque, being surrounded by a small plain, cover'd with Houses and Gardens, beyond which rise the Mountains, formerly Volcanos, but now turned into rich Vineyards, interspersed with Figtrees, Mulberries etc. The Houses are plaster'd white, with Roofs quite flat, which rising one over another, form some very pictoresque Groupes; but when one enters the Town the prospect changes, and all is filth and misery. While my Companions were drawing, I amused myself in walking towards the summet of the Island. After mounting near an hour through Vineyards, I came to bare burnt Rocks, over which I climbed with labor and difficulty, expecting to see nothing more, than barrenness and desolation; but I was suddenly surprized, on arriving to the top, by the appearance of a beautiful natural Amphitheatre of about 300. Yards diam.^{re} sunk deep amidst perpendicular Rocks, and the bottom cover'd with Vines, and a few retired Cottages. This has formerly been the Crater of the Volcano, and being surrounded by porous Rocks, it remains dry and fertile, tho' the Waters have no visible outlet.

From the highest point of these Rocks one sees all the Lipari Islands, and the Coasts of Sicily and Calabria. Immediately under one is Volcano a bare Mass of Cinders, scarcely producing a branch of Moss. It appears from hence to have been thrown up much later than most of the rest, which are of the same Material, but time has mellowed the cinders and Lava into soil, which, tho' dry is fertile and remarkably favorable to Vines.

Fazzello[15] supposes it thrown up between the second and third Punic Wars in the Consulship of Labeo and Marcellus, but this arose from mistaking a passage in Orosius,[16] which alludes to Volcanello; Volcano being mention'd by Thucydides[17] as becoming in his time; and also by Aristotle,[18] who speaks of a great eruption of this Island, which cover'd many Cities of Italy with Ashes. It was anciently call'd Thermessa & Hiera, and feigned by the Poets to be the forge of Vulcan.[19] Strabo says it burnt in three places in his time.[20] At present it burns only in one and that very little – in the course of a few thousands of years it may, according to the usual slow changes of Volcanic matter become fertile like the rest, which are probably much improved since the time of Cicero, who calls the soil of them *miserum et jejunum*.[21] Stromboli and Volcano are the only ones that burn at present, Lipari having become extinct since the time of Strabo. Its warm baths still continue much celebrated for their salubrity. Both here and in Volcano one finds great quantities of a kind of black Glass called by the naturalists Icelandish Agate, which the Ancients frequently used in sculpture.

The great effect that variations of weather have upon the fires of these Islands enables Mariners that are acquainted with them, to foretell the dangers of the Winds with great certainty; hence the fictions of the Poets about the Cave of Aeolus[22] etc. Stromboli being the highest and most exposed to the Winds, was supposed to be the place of residence of the God; hence Virgil:

– celsa sedet Aeolus arce.
    Aen. 1.[23]

He likewise takes notice of the continual noise of the Mountain and attributes it to the turbulent Winds confined in it.

Illi indignantes, magno cum murmure montis
Circum claustra fremunt. Ibid.[24]

Valerius Flaccus has described it still more particularly.

Aequore Trinacrio refugique a parte Pelori
Stat rupes horrenda fretis, quot in Aethera surgit
Molibus infernas totiens demissa sub undas,
Nec scopulos aut antra minor juxta altera tellus Cernitur.
    Arg. l. 1.[25]

Some Geographers and Antiquarians have supposed that Virgil by applying on an other occasion the Epithet *Aeolian* to the Island of Lipari, fixed the Cave of Aeolus there; but besides the evidence of Pliny[26] & Strabo,[27] the passage itself sufficiently shows the Poet's intention. The description of Flaccus is still stronger, as Stromboli is detached from the other Islands just as he describes it, whereas Lipari is closely surrounded by them. They were all sacred to Aeolus,[28] & the epithet *Aeolia* is occasionally applied to each of them. The Greek and Roman Writers reckoned only seven of these Islands, but there are at present ten. Either the three little Rocks that make up the present Number have been thrown up by subterraneous fires in later times, or were not thought worth counting.

After passing the day at Lipari, we slept in our Felucca, and set sail a little after midnight for Milazzo, anciently Myla, where we arrived in less than four hours.

[*Milazzo, April 25th*]

This Town which contains nothing remarkable, is situated upon the neck of a promontory at the extremity of a large plain, which is bounded by the Monti Montesorii call'd formerly Montes Heraei, & much celebrated for their pleasantness and fertility. The Citadel stands upon a high Rock, which commands the Town, & seems formerly to have been a place of considerable Strength. As the person to whom we were recommended lived at some distance from the Town & there was no Inn, we waited upon the Governor, who very politely provided us with a lodging. We stayed here only till the morrow morning, & then set out for Palermo with a Mulateer recommended to us by the Governor.

[*Tindaro, April 26th*][29]

After travelling along the Coast about twenty Miles, we came to a place call'd Santa Maria di Tindaro, where are still some remains of the ancient City of Tyndaris. It appears to have been

Plate 1 Charles Gore: *The Lipari Islands from the North*, 1777. Watercolour over pencil, 17.1 × 44.9 cm. Inscribed in brown ink: 'L'Isles de Stromboli, Panaria le Saline. prise du côte du Nord, douze Miles de Distance en Voyant la Stromboletta. 1777.' (Oo.4–5).

Plate 2 Charles Gore: *View of Stromboli from the North*, 1777. Watercolour and white bodycolour over pencil, 16.7 × 45.2 cm. Inscribed in brown ink: 'Stromboli du côte du nord, quatre miles eloigné. 1777. le 23 avril.' (Oo.4-6).

Plate 3 (*opposite page*) Jakob Philipp Hackert: *Temple at Segesta*, 1777. Pen and brown ink with watercolour and bodycolour over pencil, 33.3 × 44.7 cm. Inscribed in brown ink: 'Temple à Segeste en Sicile 1777 Ph. Hackert. f.' (Oo.4-7).

Plate 4 Thomas Hearne: *Ruins of the Great Temple at Selinus*, 1777. Watercolour over pencil, 23 × 37.6 cm. Signed in brown ink on a stone in the lower left-hand corner: 'Hearne' (Oo.4-13).

Plate 5 Jakob Philipp Hackert: *Ruins of the Great Temple at Selinus*, 1777. Pen and brown ink with watercolour over pencil, 23.6 × 38.6 cm (Oo.4-14).

Plate 6 Thomas Hearne: *Ruins of Selinus, from the South*, 1777. Watercolour over pencil, 28.4 × 69 cm. Signed in brown ink in the lower right-hand corner: 'THearne' (Oo.4-22).

Plate 7 Charles Gore: *The Temple of Concord at Agrigentum*, 1777. Watercolour over pencil, 24.8 × 43.4 cm. Inscribed in brown ink: 'Temple of Concord Girgenti –' (Oo.4-26).

Plate 8 Jakob Philipp Hackert: *Temple, said to be of Juno Lacinia at Agrigentum*, 1777. Pen and brown ink with watercolour over pencil, squared for transfer in pencil, 34 × 45.2 cm. Inscribed in brown ink: 'Le Temple de Junon Lucine à Girgente 1777. f. PHackert.' (Oo.4-28).

destroyed by an Earth-quake, and great part of the Hill upon which it stood, has probably faln into the Sea. The remains are the foundations of a Theatre & Temple, both seemingly of the time of the Romans. A Baron della Scuda obtained permission from the King of Naples, to dig here in search of antiquities, & I was told that he found many things of value. Probably if these researches were continued, many more might be discover'd, as this City always remained in favor & alliance with the Romans, & the Virtue & Intrepidity of one of its Citizens preserved it from the depredations of Verres,[30] who plunder'd almost every other City of Sicily.

At Tindaro we enter'd the Mountains, & about five Miles farther came to a small Tonnara, or Tunny fishery near the Town of Patti. We were obliged to pass the night here on account of a ridiculous adventure that delayed us at Patti. While our Mulateer was refreshing his Mules, my Companions amused themselves with drawing, which, they thought, they might do without the form of a permission, as there was nothing like a fortification near; But we were soon surprized by a Message from the Magistrate of Patti, who dignified himself with the title of Governor, ordering us all to appear and answer to the charges brought against us of having drawn a small watch-tower upon the coast, which he call'd a fortress. After finishing his drawing, Mr. Hackert, the principal offender, went & found the Magistrate surrounded by Lawyers who had composed an Indictment of several sheets of Paper. He told them we were only dilettanti, who travelled only for amusement, & that, had he known of any fortress, he certainly should not have ventured to draw without permission; but he was so far from thinking the tower in question one, that he had taken it for a Building to bake Earthen Pots, the making of which is the chief imployment of the Inhabitants of the Neighbourhood. The Magistrate was extremely dissatisfied with this answer; and the Lawyers all pronouncing it impossible, that we should have come so far without some very important designs, were unanimous for detaining us, when Mr. Hackert took some Letters from his Pocket, which he desired them to read. These being recommendations to the Vice-roy & several of the principal People of the Island, threw the whole process into confusion, & he was dismissed with a number of apologies for the trouble they had given him.[31]

From hence we pursued our journey along the Shore, and sometimes among the Mountains. Thro' the worst roads I never travelled, but the richness & beauty of the Country made ample amends for every inconvenience of this kind.

We found the Heraean Mountains well worthy of the encomiums bestowed upon them by Diodorus.[32] In some places they are broken into the most beautiful & romantic forms, the sides cover'd with rich Groves of Olives and Oaks, & the tops with Towns and Villages. In others vast terraces rise one above another, some cultivated & planted with Vines, Figtrees & Mulberries, others hung with those Shrubs, which in England are kept in Greenhouses, with so much care & Labor, & which here florish in all the wild luxuriance of Nature, & cloath the rugged Rocks with perpetual Verdure.

In these Mountains are great varieties of beautiful Marbles, among which I observed a kind of red Porphyry, coarser & less hard & solid than the Antique. Probably, if the Quarries were opened, it might be found of a better quality deep in the Rock, as the pieces I saw, were only fragments detached from the surface, & consequently much injured by having been always exposed to Wind & Water.

[*Aquadolce*]

At night we arrived at Aquadolce, a little Village, which takes its Name from a source of fresh Water in the Sea about half a mile from the shore. The Village is maintained by this Spring, as the Fish come constantly to it, & the Inhabitants are engaged in a Society to take & divide them. Directly above Aquadolce rises a high Mountain, on the top of which was the Ancient City of Aluntium,[33] of which there are no remains. At the bottom of it towards the Sea, is a large Cave composed of the same Materials as that already mentioned near Cape Palinuro, except that one finds mixed with the bones & Gravel, Seashells & particles of calcined Matter. The bony petrifactions are also in much greater quantity, & appear, as I was told by the Peasants, in other parts of the Mountain. We walked into the Cavern about 100. Yards, where it became so rugged and narrow, that we could go no farther, but our Guide told us, that he had driven a Cat in, which came out at a Cavern on the other side of the Mountain, three miles distant.

From hence we came by the fortress of Tusa to Lufinali, a miserable Inn, where we were obliged to pass the night.

[*Cefalu*]

On the morrow we dined at Cefalu, formerly Cephaladis,[34] & slept at Termine formerly Thermae Himerenses. Fazzello (who wrote under Charles 5.th) mentions ruins that existed in his time both of Alusa & Cephaladis;[35] but I could neither see nor hear any thing of them. The latter is now a considerable Town, situated at the Point of a Promontory under a high craggy Mountain, upon the summet of which is the Citadel, which, if well fortified would be impregnable.

[*Termini*]

The Baths at Termini are still much in use, but there are no remains either of Himera or the ancient Therma. The salubrious effects of these Baths are attributed to St. Cologus, who was a Physician, and had the good luck to get the Reputation of a Saint instead of a Wizzard.

The Ancients, who were little less fond of Miracles than the Moderns, & much more ingenious in inventing them, feigned that the Nymphs opened them at the Instigation of Minerva, to refresh Hercules during his expedition thro' Sicily.

[*Himera*][36]

Himera stood on the other side of the river of the same name about half a mile from Termine. It is mentioned by Thucidydes[37] among the principal Cities of Sicily, but being taken by the Carthaginians about 400. years before the Christian Aera, Annibal, their General order'd it to be totally destroyed to avenge the death of his Grand-father, who was defeated & killed here, by the confederate forces of Syracuse Agrigentum & Himera.[38]

After the destruction of Carthage, Scipio[39] established the scatter'd remains of the Himereans at Therma, & gave them the Statues etc. which the Carthaginians had formerly carried away. Among these were two of Brass of excellent Workmanship,

13 Thomas Hearne: *View of the Citadel of Cefalù*, 1777. Watercolour over pencil, 27.1 × 44.9 cm. Inscribed in brown ink: 'View of Cephalu North Coast of Sicily between Milazzo & Pale[rmo]' (Oo.4-41).

mention'd by Cicero to have been carried away by Verres, one representing Stesicorus, the Poet,[40] who was of this City, & the other an allegorical figure of the City itself.[41]

[*La Bagaria*]

From Termine to Palermo is twenty four miles. About half Way we came to a Villa called la Bagaria,[42] lately built by a Prince Palagonia. It is the most singular structure I ever saw, & cover'd both within & without by the most extravagant figures that it is possible to imagine. The Gardens are in the same Stile & I believe it would be difficult to form an Idea of a Monster that is not to be found here. The greatest part are executed in a rough kind of Stone, some in plaster & some in Marble. There are many hundreds of them, which were continually increasing, but the Prince's Relations prevailed upon the Government, to put his estate under the care of Trustees, that he might not totally ruin himself by this absurd taste.

[*Palermo, May 1st*]

We arrived at Palermo May 1st. The situation of it is very beautiful in a small but fertile Vale surrounded by barren Mountains. The Streets are regular & clean, & the general appearance rich & populous, but the Architecture extremely bad: Prince Palagonia's taste seems to prevail thro' the whole City.[43]

We found the People during the short time we stayed here, exceedingly civil. They affect none of that unwieldy greatness, which the Roman and Neapolitan Nobility assume, but seem to study more the real enjoyments of Life. Strangers are sure of meeting with attention & civility, & that in the most pleasing kind, for their manner of living is very easy & polite. They have their *conversationi* or Assemblies like the Italians, but more agreeable, as the Women are not coupled each with a *Cavalier servante*. There is one at the Viceroys Palace every night, except Thursday and Friday, when they only receive particular people. Before going to the Assemblies they meet upon the Quay, which is a kind of Mill. During the summer they pass the evening in walking about there & have Music, refreshments etc. The Ladies have lately found it convenient to introduce a very singular regulation, which is that all torches are extinguished before the carriages come upon the Quay, to prevent any disagreeable discoveries, for it seems that some Men here are still so unreasonable, to expect fidelity from their Wives. These expectations indeed, are generally vain, for the Constitutions of the Sicilians are too warm, to resist opportunity, which is never wanting here. The Women are in general lively & agreeable, but destitute of that [sic] accomplishments, which render our own fair Country-Women so amiable. They are married extremely young, & those that are not under the necessity of exposing themselves to the burning rays of the Sun, are rather handsome. Their Manners are not extremely polished, but easy & natural, & not spoiled by that awkward imitation of the French, which renders the Italians so ridiculous; and from which the Inhabitants of our own Country are not totally free.

During the month of May they have a fair in the Piazza del Domo, which exhibits a very singular scene. The square is illuminated & surrounded by Shops for toys, trinkets etc. with a Lottery in the Middle. It opens about sunset, & continues till Midnight. The whole Town assemble here and are all upon an equality – Princes and Coblers, Princesses & Milleners are upon the same footing, and mix undistinguished in the Crowd. It may be imagined that such excellent conveniency for pleasure & debauchery are not neglected by People so lively as the Sicilians.

The objects of curiosity in Palermo are not very numerous. The Port is to the west of the City, and contains nothing remarkable. Immediately beyond it is Mount Eryx now called Monte Pelegrino, & celebrated for the Church of St. Rosalia, the tutelary Saint of the Palermitans. This is said to be the Mountain upon which Amilcar defended himself with so much bravery and perseverance during the first Punic War.[44] The form of it answers exactly to the description of Polybius,[45] but I could find no traces of the Carthaginian Camp. The supposed Body of St. Rosalia was formed [sic] in a Cave near the summit of the Mountain, where the Church now is. It was probably the Body of some Carthaginian who little expected ever to have been treated with divine honors.

In the College formerly belonging to the Jesuites are a good Collection of Etruscan Vases, some fossils, a good Bust of Plato & another of Tiberius. The Gems and Medals, of which, it is said, here was a good collection, were all carried away by the Jesuits before their Abolishment.

14 Charles Gore: *View of Palermo* (Weimar, Goethe-Nationalmuseum).

The Viceroy's Palace is an old irregular fabric, built at different times.[46] The Chapel[47] seems to be as early as the Greek Emperors, as it is cover'd within & without with a kind of barbarous Mosaic like the Churches in Rome, that were built by those Princes. In the Gallery are the portraits of all the Kings of Sicily, beginning with Ruggiero the first of the Roman Race.

There are also two Rams of Brass, brought from Syracuse; they are somewhat larger than the life, and of the most exquisite Sculpture.[48] It is astonishing what an Air of dignity & grandeur the Artist has given to so humble an Animal, & yet preserved the exactitude of a portrait. The finishing is in that bold masterly Stile, which is peculiar to the best ages of Greece. – Even in the turn of the Horns there is Grace & elegance, & the Wool tho' seemingly neglected has all the softness & lightness of Nature. Upon the whole these Bronzes are equal if not superior to any thing I have seen at Rome, Portici, or Florence, & may be ranked among the few genuine Works that exist of the fine Greek Artists. They are both after the same design, but the one is much superior to the other. Fazzinello says they were placed upon the Gates of the fortress of Ortygia by Georgius Maniaces, General of the Emperor Constantine Monomacus & were supposed to have been brought from Constantinople,[49] tho' I should rather suppose them to be remains of ancient Syracusan taste & Magnificence.

[Montreale, May 5th]

May the 5th we left Palermo and went to Alcamo, about 30. Miles distant.

As far as Montreale, the Road is very magnificent, & was made at the expense of the late Archbishop of that place,[50] who imployed his immense Revenues in a manner much applauded but little imitated by his Brethren. Instead of squandering them in pageantry & ostentation, or saving them for worthless Relations, he lived with the simplicity of a Hermit, & imployed his wealth in works of real Charity; not in incouraging Idleness and beggary but in imploying the industrious poor in works of public ornament & utility.

The Town of Montreale is small but situated upon a beautiful Bank, that commands the Vale and City of Palermo. The Cathedral[51] seems to be of the time of the Greek Emperors being much ornamented with that barbarous kind of Mosaic, so much used in those ages. There are a number of rich porphyry Columns finished in a Stile half Gothic, & a magnificent sarcophagus of the same Material, containing the Body of William 1st King of Sicily.[52] This Porphyry is equal in quality to any that has been found in Rome, & seems to prove, that the Romans drew a great part of what they used from Sicily, tho' all is supposed to have come from Africa. The form and workmanship of the columns prove them to have been made after the Sarazins had seized upon that Part of the Roman Empire, & the Death of King William happened in 1100, an age so barbarous, that all external Commerce was unknown.

[Aegesta or Segesta, May 6th][53]

At Alcamo we lay in the Castle & went the morrow morning to view the ruins of Aegesta or Segesta eight miles distant. On approaching one is struck with a view of a noble temple, which stands alone upon a small Hill surrounded by high Mountains.

It has six columns in front and fourteen deep, all entire with their entablatures. The Architecture is the old Doric, but it appears never to have been finished, the Shafts of the columns being only rough hewn. I could find no foundations of the cell,[54] & am inclined to think that it was never built, as there were a number of square stones near, probably intended for that purpose. The Columns are about 6. feet diam.^r but their being unfinished renders it impossible to tell their just dimensions. The intablature[55] I could not measure, not being able to procure a Ladder & there were no fragments on the Ground. This Temple stood without the Walls of the City, which was situated upon the Hill opposite its eastern front, where are still remaining a great many fragments, & foundations of Buildings & a Theatre half-ruined. It is built of hewn Stone without cement, & like all the Greek Theatres upon a declivity, so that the back seats rest upon the ground. As near as I could measure amidst the Shrubs and ruins with which it was cover'd, it was about 200. feet wide. The Steps had been all carried away, or thrown down, & there were no remains of the Podium, or Proscenium. Its aspect is towards the Sea & the view from it very fine, commanding almost all the Country of the Elymi.

The City of Aegesta, or, as the Romans named it, Segesta, was according to Virgil built by the Trojans:

Interea Aeneas urbem designat aratro
Sortiturque domos; hoc Ilium et haec loca Troja
Esse jubet.[56]

It was named by Aeneas in honor of his host Acestes,[57] & the little Streams that flow under it, were called Simois & Scamander. It afterwards became a powerful Republic, but was taken & plunder'd by the Carthaginians, whom the Aegestans themselves had invited into Sicily. It recover'd after this, but was again taken & totally destroyed by Agathocles.[58] When the Romans became Masters of Sicily, they restored it, out of respect to their common origin, & favor'd it with many privileges, but it never seems to have rose to any great Splendor, as the buildings that remain are evidently of the very earliest times. The warm Springs are a little below the City, upon the banks of the Scamander, now S.^{to} Bartolomeo, but are totally neglected.

After spending the day at Aegesta, we went to Calatafini, a small Town three Miles distant, where we passed the night.

[Selinus][59]

Finding that there were no remains of Eryx[60] or Lilybaeum, nor anything curious in the neighborhood of Drapani or Trappani, we went directly to Castelvetrano, & from thence the same day to the Ruins of Selinus, where we lay in a little Watch-Tower, the only habitation now existing where once stood that mighty City.

We found here six magnificent Temples,[61] all prostrate upon the ground, but the parts sufficiently intire to show what they once were. The three eastern ones stood upon a small eminence without the Walls, in a line from North to South, about 200. yards from the Sea. The largest & most northern of them was according to Herodotus[62] dedicated to Jupiter Forensis and according to Pausanias[63] to Jupiter Olympius. The stupendous Ruins of it, which still cover a great share of ground, prove it to have been one of the most magnificent Edifices ever built. It had eight columns in front and seventeen deep, each ten feet diam.^r at base & six at the Capital, & about fifty feet high. Each round is a single Stone of which there are seldom more than eight in a Column, & in many less. The Capitals are like those of the great Temple or Basilica at Paestum & the Columns diminished regularly from bottom to top. The Abacus is twelve feet, ten Inches square, & the trigliffs[64] four feet long and every other number of the entablature in proportion. The intercolumnation[65] was a little more than a diametre, but the ruins are tumbled into such confused heaps, that I could not measure with exactitude. It appears never to have been quite finished, as some of the columns are fluted, & some plain & others fluted a little way from the Capitals. There are also some pieces of the Architrave lying at a considerable distance which seem never to have been set. These are of an immense size, each Stone in the Architrave being twenty feet and a half long, seven feet high and five broad.

The next Temple is of the same Architecture, but much smaller having only six columns in front and fourteen deep, & these not above five feet diametre. The third is larger than the second but much smaller than the first, & is probably the most ancient of the three, as the columns are proportionably shorter, & the Capitals of a different form. Like most of this order it had six in front and fourteen deep. Their diametre was about seven feet six inches at base, and about five feet six inches at top and the height about four Diametres. In all three temples each column has twenty flutes, as is usual in the old Doric Buildings.

A few hundred yards to the West was the ancient Port which is now filled with Sand, but the ruins of the Quay are still visible. Upon the Bank beyond it stood the City, the ruins of which consisting of foundations and fragments of different edifices, cover a great extent.

Near the Sea are the remains of three more temples, in the same state as those already described. Two of them were of the usual proportion, & nearly the same in every respect with the least of the others. The third had six columns in front and fifteen deep, & only sixteen flutes in each column – in other respects it resembled the rest. They are all of the old Doric order without Bases, & were probably built at no great distance of time, as the prosperity of that city was of very short duration. It was built by a Colony from Megara, about 640. years before the Christian Aera, & soon became one of the most powerful States of Sicily; but being engaged in a War with the Aegestans, the latter called the Carthaginians to their assistance, who sent a powerful Army of Mercenaries under the Command of Annibal, whose father Giseo had been killed, while in exile at Selinus.[66] The Greeks enervated by Luxury & elegance were unable to keep the field against the hardy Barbarians of Spain & Africa, but being skilled in the arts of defence, they supported a long siege with great bravery and perseverance. However the City was at length taken by Storm, and totally destroy'd. The Inhabitants were either killed or sold for Slaves. – 3000. of them were sacrificed by Annibal, at the tomb of his father. The Temples, the most beautiful & magnificent in Sicily, were thrown down, & when the Syracusians sent Ambassadors to beg that they might be spared, Annibal replied that the Gods, to his certain knowledge, had left them, & it was better that they should be destroyed than put to profane uses.

Thus fell Selinus about 240. years after its foundation, a memorable monument of the vanity & greatness of human Genius & Industry. Perhaps of all buildings that have ever been erected in the World, the great Temple of Selinus (next to the Pyramids of Egypt) [was] the best calculated for duration; but by the destructive Ambition of a neighboring State it was thrown down almost at the moment of being finished. Even this Calamity could not totally destroy it, for its ruins still remain testimony of its greatness, when those of Carthage have long since perished.

This unfortunate City was partly rebuilt by those who had escaped the siege and preserved a precarious existence for about 150. years, when it was again taken and finally destroyed by the Carthaginians. Strabo mentions it as being totally deserted in his time,[67] & it is probable that the Temples are now in the same state, as they were left by Annibal, except that many of the fragments have been carried away & used in modern buildings. Some have supposed from the confused state in which they lay, that they must have been thrown down by an Earth-quake. It is indeed difficult to conceive how any man should have imployed so much labor and ingenuity as the ruin of these vast edifices must have required purely to gratify a wanton love of destroying; But besides the Testimony of Diodorus[68] the Temples themselves appear upon a close examination to have been thrown down by design. The Columns of the larger ones have all fallen one way and seem to have been undermined. The smallest ones were probably pulled down by military Engines, as the bottom piece of each column still stands in its place. In what manner soever they were destroyed it must have been with great labor & difficulty, for the foundations are immensely deep, & the whole

15 Charles Gore:
The Ruins of Selinus
(Weimar, Goethe-Nationalmuseum).

built with a greatness & stability that surpass even the noblest works of the Roman Emperors. So much the more wonderful as they were the production of a Republic, that existed but a short time, & which was never much more than a trading Company. While one views them, one cannot but reflect how inestimable is the blessing of Liberty, that enabled so small a State as Selinus, whose dominions extended but a few miles to perform what the mighty Lords of the Earth have scarcely equalled.

About six Miles from Selinus are the Latomiae, or Stone quarries in which are still immense pieces of unfinished Columns, Architraves etc. which the untimely fall of the City prevented from being imployed. The Country round is now dry and barren, tho' flat. It is probably much altered since the time of the Greeks, from the petrifying quality of the Waters. Virgil calls it *palmosa Selinus*,[69] but at present there is no single palm tree to be seen. Its modern name is *terra delle pulci*,[70] which we found has not been given without reason, for the Tower was so full of them, that we were almost devoured.

The room in which we lay has occasionally served for one of those convenient places, where a despotic Prince or Minister can destroy an obnoxious person, without the formality of a tryal, or parade of a public execution. The air being extremely poisonous during the Summer months, a very short confinement is sufficient to quiet the most turbulent Patriot.

[*Sciacca, May 10th*]

We stay'd here two days to draw and measure the ruins and then went to *Sciacca*, formerly Therma Selinuntia. The hot Baths & mineral Waters are still much in use, but what makes this place much frequented from all parts of Sicily, is a *Sudatorium* or *Stuffo* upon the top of a Mountain near the Town. This is a natural cavern in the Rock, from which issues with great violence a hot Stream, which has been found to be of great benefit in cases of Gout, Rheumatism etc. The patient sits in it for about half an hour, & then goes to bed, & repeats the same every day till he is cured. The cavern has been much enlarged by Art, and furnished with a number of seats cut out of the Rock. It was anciently supposed to be the work of Daedalus; but the Moderns attribute it to St. Calogus, in spite of the evidence of its having existed so many ages before any of their Saints were thought of.

[*Girgenti or Agrigento*][71]

From hence we came to Girgenti, where we were hospitably received by the Franciscans. This City stands very high upon the declivity of a Hill, where stood the Citadel of ancient Agrigentum. It commands a beautiful view to the northwest over the Ground where that famous City stood, which is now planted with Olives & other trees, interspersed with Ruins, of which here are in greater quantities & better preserved than any where else in Sicily.

There are some remains of about fourteen Temples, all of the old Doric order, with great numbers of Sepulcral Grotto's, Magazins for Grain, hollowed in the Rock etc. The first, beginning from the East, is the Temple of Juno Lucina,[72] of which remain the basement, a small part of the Cell, and about half the Portico. The Columns are about 4 ft. 3 In. diam.^{re} at bottom & about 3. ft. 15 In. at top, diminished regularly like those of

Selinus. The entablature seemed much the same, as in other Temples of the old Doric order, but it was so much mutilated, that I could not measure it with any exactitude. The Agrigentine Stone being a soft sandy petrifaction, very subject to moulder, the smaller parts are scarcely distinguishable in any of these buildings. The present appearance of the Temple of Juno is the most picturesque that can be imagined. It is situated upon a small Hill, cover'd with trees, among which lie the broken Columns etc. that have fallen down, for the material is so coarse that they are not thought worth carrying away.

Next to the Temple of Juno is that of Concord,[73] of the same size & place, and only differing in some insignificant ornaments. Part of the Cell of it is converted into a Church, and all the Columns with the greatest part of the entablature, remain, tho' much corroded by time & vicissitudes of weather.

The Temple of Hercules,[74] which appears next is much larger than either of the former, but the shape & proportions of it were nearly the same. There is only one Column standing – the rest are all lying in the places where they fell. Their diametre was about six feet six inches, and height about five diametres. – The entablature was too much decayed to be made out. In this Temple was the famous Statue of Hercules, which Verres attemted to carry away but was prevented by the Spirit and Activity of the Agrigentines.[75]

A little further was the celebrated Temple of Jupiter Olympius, described by Diodorus Siculus.[76] There at present remain only a few fragments which are however sufficient to show its stupendous size, in which it surpassed even that of Selinus tho' much inferior to it in beauty of design and magnificence of execution. It had eight semicolumns in front & seventeen on each side. These were 10f.t 2 In. diam.re at top. What was their size at bottom I could not discover, for the Shafts were built with small Stones, like those of the front portico of St. Peter's at Rome & are entirely moulder'd into dust. The general dimensions of the Temple given by Diodorus are 360. feet long, 120. high and 60. broad.[77] In the two first he seems to have been nearly exact, but in the breadth he has mistaken exactly 100 f.t as appears plainly from the foundations.

In the Pediment of the eastern Portico was the battle of the

16 Jakob Philipp Hackert: *Temple of Hercules at Agrigentum*, 1777. Pen and brown ink with brown wash over traces of pencil, 34.1 × 45.5 cm. Inscribed in brown ink: 'Temple d'hercule a Girgente 1777. Ph. Hackert f.' (Oo.4-27).

Giants, & in the western the taking of Troy, both of the finest Sculpture,[78] that one of the most wealthy and magnificent of all Grecian Cities could produce in a time, when the Arts were at the highest pitch of perfection. Like many of the great Works of the Greeks it was never finished. Their daring Genius was forever aiming at the sublime, but few of them had the ability to put their vast plans into execution. They were besides divided into a number of little States, and drawn onto these immense undertakings by mutual jealousy & emulation. Happy had it been for them, if they had never endeavored to show their superiority over each other by any more destructive way, nor engaged in Wars, which obliged the Vanquished to fly for assistance to foreign Nations, who in a short time reduced both their Friends and Enemies to an equal state of servitude. A great part of the Temple of Jupiter Olympius was standing till the year 1494. when it suddenly fell down without any visible cause.

Of the Temple of Vulcan there are two mutilated Columns remaining, with their substructions. It appears to have been exactly the same as those of Juno Lucina and Concord. There are also two Semicolumns and part of the Wall of the Temple of Aesculapius, where was the famous Statue of Apollo mentioned by Cicero.[79] Of the others there is scarce any thing left but foundations.

I have mention'd them all under the names, by which they are known at present, tho' except those of Jupiter Olympius, Vulcan & Aesculapius, they have been named from very dubious Authority.

Between the ancient City & the River Hypsa is a small pyramidal Building said to be the Tomb of Hiero.[80] It is raised upon a pedestal and has an Ionic Column, fluted, projected from each Angle, but the Entablature is Doric. Whether this Edifice is of a date anterior to the perfection, or after the decline of Architecture in Sicily, seems doubtful. I am inclined to think the latter, as it is much too neat & pretty for the Age of Hieron.

There are some other fragments of the time of the Romans, particularly a rich piece of Corinthian Cornice of white Marble, now hollowed & used as a Cistern. It appears to have belonged to a circular Building of great magnificence.

The City Walls may still be traced in a circuit of about 10. Miles. In some places they are cut out of the Rock, & full of niches in which were placed the Ashes of the Dead. I have not observed this method of burial any where else, & cannot imagine what was their Motive for it, except they meant it as an honorable distinction for those, who died for their Country or thought, by placing the Ashes in the Walls, to interest the Manes[81] in their defence. The Common Sewers are still visible in many parts, and appear to have been made with great Labor & expence, being cut out of the solid Rock and large enough for a Man to walk thro'. The ground between the ancient and modern City is intirely filled with square holes sunk in the Rock and cover'd with flat Stones, probably the sepulcres of the Slaves or poorer Citizens.

Agrigentum was once the largest City of Sicily, except Syracuse, & is said to have contained 200,000 Inhabitants. According to the extent of the Walls, this Computation must have been much too small, & probably excluded the Slaves, who in the ancient Republics at least doubled the number of the freemen. The Agrigentines were famous for their luxury, elegance, magnificence and hospitality, hence Empedocles[82] used to say, that they ate and drank as if they were to die to-morrow, and built as if they were to live for ever.

This luxury and refinement soon proved their destruction, for

17 Thomas Hearne: *The Sepulchre at Agrigentum*, 1777. Pen and grey-brown ink with watercolour over pencil, 27 × 44.7 cm. Signed in brown ink in the lower left-hand corner: 'THearne' (Oo.4–23).

about 400. years before the Christian aera it was besieged and taken by Hamilcar, the Carthaginian, who stripped it of all its superb ornaments and carried them to Carthage. It afterwards regained its liberty but never again its ancient Splendor. During the second Punic War it was taken by the Romans & suffer'd much for having favor'd the Carthaginians. After the destruction of Carthage Scipio restored to it all its ancient ornaments, which Hamilcar had carried away. Among them was the famous Bull of Brass made by Perillus and presented to the Tyrant Phaleris.[83] The conduct of Scipio in this was extremely politic, as it at once shewed the Sicilians a monument of the Cruelty of their own Princes, of the capacity of the Carthaginians, and the moderation of the Romans. This moderation lasted but a short time. Soon after Carthage was destroyed, when they had no rival to fear, the whole impire was pillaged by their Consuls and Praetors.

Inde Dolabella est, atque hinc Antonius, inde
Sacrilegus Verres: referebant navibus altis
Occulta spolia, et plures de pace triumphos.
Nunc sociis juga pauca boum, grex paruces equarum,
Et pater armenti capto eripiatur agello:
Ipsi deinde Lares, si quod spectabile signum
Si quis in aedicula Deus unicus.
    Juv. Sat. 8[84]

Such is the description of a Poet who speaks too often truth.

Diodorus mentions Agrigentum as being in his time in a state of decay.[85] It probably continued declining, till the time of Queen Constance,[86] when the present City of Girgenti sprung from its ruins. This now contains about 12000. Inhabitants who carry on a considerable trade in corn. The Houses are poor and ill-built, almost all the wealth of the Country belonging to the Church. The Archbishop alone has an Income of near 20 000. £ Sterling p.^r annum, which is a constant drain for the Country, for he never resides there. His Palace is large, but in a very bad taste. It has a magnificent Library, furnished with a great many books of Antiquities and Divinity but very little else. There is likewise a Cabinet of Medals, among which are some good Sicilian and Punic ones.

In the Cathedral Church is a large Marble Sarcophagus,[87] which now serves for the baptismal fount. It is adorned with alto-relievos on each side, which have occasioned much dispute among the learned & Idle of Girgenti. Some maintain that it was the sepulcre of Phaleris the first, and others of Phintias the last Tyrant of Agrigentum. Both these opinions have given rise to very long treatises in which they are supported by Arguments equally frivolous and ingenious. The shape and size of it resemble that of Julia Mammaea and Alexander Severus[88] at Rome. The Sculpture is much in the same Stile, perhaps not so good, tho' the Girgentines, who never saw any thing better, esteem it as a prodigy of Art, and have persuaded some travellers, who judge more by their Ears than by their Eyes, to be of the same opinion. It appears to one to be Roman, & probably contained the Ashes of some Consul or Praetor under the Emperors. The Sculptures seem to have represented some particular Circumstances of his life and family now unknown, which the natural love of mystery and refinement, has construed into remote meanings of Allegory and Mythology.

We found the Inhabitants of Girgenti extremely civil and willing to oblige. They value themselves much upon the reputation of their Ancestors for hospitality & kindness to Strangers, which they endeavour to imitate as far as the difference of their circumstances will permit: But however amiable and commendable their intention may be, it rather incommodes than assists a

Stranger, for attention and civility become tiresome and impertinent, when those who show it have neither wit to amuse, nor knowledge to instruct. This is too much the case with the Girgentines as well as the rest of the Sicilians. Their natural vivacity of Temper renders them busy & inquisitive, & thro' a want of education, they become rude and impertinent. One is sorry to be under the necessity of rejecting Civilities, that are offer'd with an intention to please, and yet one cannot suffer all one's time to be wasted in answering frivolous questions, and listening to unmeaning remarks.

The territory of Girgenti is fertile in Corn & Olives but all the Sicilian oil, through a want of skill in making it, is very bad. It likewise breeds excellent Horses, for which it was anciently celebrated

Arduus inde Acragas ostentat maxima longe
Moenia, magnanimûm quondam generator equorum.
    Aen.[89]

[Alicata, May 17th]

May 17th we went from Girgenti to Alicata, and on the morrow to Biscara. We could find no remains of Gela or Camerina, tho' Fazzello and Cluverius[90] mention some that existed in their time.

The *Campi Geloi*, which extend all the way between Alicata and Terranuova, are extremely fertile, but like all this Coast, very ill cultivated. The Lake which formerly render'd Camarina unwholesome, now poisons the Country round it, which is naturally exceedingly rich. It was formerly called the palus Camarina. – The City being once afflicted with a Plague, consulted the Oracle of Apollo, whether they should drain it, but were commanded, not to move Camarina. Not comprehending the meaning of this answer, they drained the Lake, which cured the Plague, but gave the Enemy an opportunity of entering the Town; hence Virgil:

Fatis nunquam concessa moveri
Adparet Camarina procul –
    Aen. 3[91]

We found the Hypparis and Oanus miserable little Rivulets, that would never have been noted had not Pindar dignified them with his Verses.[92]

[Biscari, May 17th]

At Biscari we perceived an agreeable change in the Country. The fields were richly cultivated and newly enclosed; the banks planted with Vines & Mulberries; & every thing wore the face of prosperity and improvement. We found upon inquiry that this was the Estate of Prince Biscari, and that all the improvements were owing to his Spirit and generosity. We were but too soon convinced of the truth of this; for the moment we were out of his estate, the signs of misery & Idleness again appeared, and continued all the Way to Syracuse. This Coast, which once maintained so many florishing Cities in all the elegances and luxuries of life, can scarcely now produce necessaries for its miserable Inhabitants. Bigotry and oppression and a false system of political economy have done more in laying waste Sicily, than the worst effects of War & tumult could have produced. The same system has extended its fatal influence over all the vast Monarchy of Spain. While the other Nations of Europe encouraged Arts and manufactures, the Spaniards imployed themselves in remote conquests, which they endeavored to preserve by rendering them poor and dependent. Their Monarchy became by this means an immense unwieldy Body, composed of a number of unconnected parts, equally feeble and uncapable of assisting each other. The vast treasures, that flow to them from the Indies, come and go like a torrent, leaving nothing but waste and desolation behind. They are only received by a few and even those are but momentary Possessors, who immediately imploy them in procuring foreign Luxuries, the productions of the Ingenious & Laborious. Thus the Spaniards are only the Bankers for the rest of the World, ever in possession of immense treasures, and yet poor.

The Wealth of a Nation consists in the number of Industrious Inhabitants, and not in the quantity of Gold or Silver. For this naturally comes, where there is the former. When it is thus acquired, it animates and inspires every thing, – ease and affluence being in the power of each individual to procure, a general Spirit of emulation appears. The husbandman and manufacturer are equally bent upon improvement, and every one is imployed in endeavoring to acquire that wealth, which he thinks will enable him to end his life in the enjoyment of ease and pleasure.

[Syracuse, May 20th][93]

May 20th. we arrived at the once famous City of Syracuse, now again confined to the Island of Ortygia, which in the time of its greatness was only the smallest of its four divisions. A great part even of that is occupied by the fortifications, which are exceedingly strong & extensive; &, considering that they belong to the King of Naples, in very good order. We went immediately to view the fountain of Arethusa,[94] which still flows in abundance; but the prayer of Virgil

(Sic tibi, cum fluctus subterlabere Sicanos,
Doris amara suam non intermisceat undam)[95]

has not prevail'd, for since the Earth-quake of 1693. it has been brackish, & only served for a Wash-pool. We found it frequented by Nymphs somewhat different from those described by Theocritus and Virgil,[96] – no other than a company of the most dirty old washer-women, I ever beheld.

The Cathedral Church is an old Doric Temple, supposed, but without any Authority, to be that of Minerva, so celebrated for its wealth and Magnificence. It is still tolerably intire, but so cover'd and disguised by modern ornaments, that the ancient form is totally lost.

Of the Theatre and Amphitheatre there remains nothing but some inconsiderable foundations and the Seats cut in the Rock. Upon one of those of the Theatre is inscribed: ΒΑΣΙΛΙΣΣΑΣ ΦΙΛΙΣΤΙΔΟΣ[97] which, some have supposed, relates to a Queen, of whom History has left no record. In confirmation of this they bring a Medal, inscribed Β.Φ. which they attribute to the same Queen.[98] Others say the Caracters are of too modern a Shape to have been of an Age beyond the reach of History. Like most disputes of this nature, it furnishes a very innocent amusement to the Idle and inquisitive, in which Sicily is very fertile.

Not far from the Theatre are the Latomiae of Epipola,[99] which were anciently the Public Prisons. They are immense quarries of Stone, sunk to a great depth & in some places hollowed into immense Vaults supported by Pillars, hewn out of the Rock. Many of these have given way and enormous Masses have faln down, which being cover'd with Shrubs and herbage form the

18 Charles Gore and Thomas Hearne: *View of Syracuse from Epipolie*, 1777. Watercolour over pencil, heightened with white, 27.4 × 44.2 cm (Oo.4-37).

19 Jakob Philipp Hackert: *View of a Quarry at Syracuse*, 1777. Pen and brown ink with brown wash over pencil, 34.4 × 46.7 cm. Inscribed in brown ink: 'Latomie de Siracuse 1777.' and signed in the foreground 'Ph. Hackert.' (Oo.4-36).

most wild and beautiful Scene that can be imagined. In one of these Caverns is a Manufactory of Saltpetre, which heightens its natural gloominess. The Smoke of the furnace, the dim light of the fire, and black visages of the People made it look like some enchanted Scene of a Romance.

What is call'd the Ear of Dionysius[100] is a Cavern about 60 feet high & about 130. wide, narrowed almost to a point at the top. It goes into the Rock about 70. yards, in the shape of an S, & has still a very strong Echo, tho' probably much weakened by a modern excavation, that has been made on one side. The Story of its having been made by Dionysius to discover the secrets of the prisoners, is probably of more modern invention, as I do not find it mention'd by any ancient Author. The Echo appears however designed, for the cavern is formed with much more Art and care than any of the rest. It might perhaps have been intended to discover any tumult or insurrection among the Prisoners. There are the foundations of some building over the mouth of it, which may possibly have been the Keeper's House, as here any noise from within must have been distinctly heard. Aelian[101] says that the most beautiful of the Caverns in the Latomiae was called after the name of Philoxenus[102] the Poet, who wrote his Poem of the Cyclops while confined there by Dionysius. I am inclined to believe this the Cavern of Philoxenus, as it is much superior to the rest both in grandeur, beauty & regularity.

The Latomiae of Acridina are nearer the Sea, and are now the Gardens of a Capuchin Convent. They are in the same stile

20 Jakob Philipp Hackert and Thomas Hearne: *Cavern, called the 'Ear of Dionysius' at Syracuse*, 1777. Watercolour over pencil, 44.4 × 27.5 cm. Inscribed in grey ink: 'Orecchio di Dionysio a Syracusa' (Oo.4-35).

as the others, but still more beautiful and pictoresque. The immense Caverns and broken Rocks are richly hung with Vines & the Bottom planted with Fig trees, Oranges and Pomegranates. What they were formerly one may judge from the description of Cicero:

Opus est ingens, magnificum regum ac tyrannorum, totum maltorum opere penitus exercisum. Nihil tam clausum ad exitus, nihil tam tutum ad custodias nec fieri, *nec cogitari potest*.[103]

Thus are these tremendous Palaces of Vengeance, on[c]e the Receptacles of crimes and misery, become the most delightful Spots upon earth, & the gloomy Caves, where so many Wretches have linger'd away their Lives in horror and despair, now form the most pleasing and romantic retreats, equally guarded from the heats of Summer or colds of Winter.

On the other side of the Anapus are two mutilated Columns, supposed to be the remains of the temple of Jupiter Olympius, to which the Athenians retreated after their repulse from Syracuse.[104] They have only 16. flutes and are the first of the old Doric order, that I have seen with Bases. Till lately there were much more considerable remains of this temple, & in a very short time there will be none at all, as the peasants are continually carrying away the Stones to build with. These with some subterraneous Aquaducts and sepulcral Grotto's are all the remains of the mighty City of Syracuse, once so exquisitely beautiful, that e'en Marcellus[105] in the Career of his Conquests could not help bursting into tears and cursing the fatal lust of Empire, that obliged him to ruin the Glory and envy of the Universe. The sumptuous Palaces of Dionysius and Hiero,[106] with all the noble Works of Sculpture and painting that adorned them, are destroyed and not a vestige of them left behind. Even the Walls, whose strength and magnificence were the wonder of the Romans, have so totally perished, that one cannot trace the foundations of them.

When one reads the accounts of all these vast works one wonders, how they could have been so nearly annihilated, but when one considers the number of calamities, which the City has undergone, how often it has been pillaged, sacked and burnt, one equally wonders, that they are not entirely so. The Inhabitants were as celebrated for luxury & magnificence, as their buildings for grandeur and stability. The mensae Syracusanae were famous thro' all the world, & the feasts of Dionysius and Hiero still seem incredible. But all their wealth and magnificence could not defend them from a few hardy Robbers, who sallying from their thatched Cottages, where they had been inured to labor and severity, easily took possession of the sumptuous Palaces of the refined and enervated Greeks.

The great port of Syracuse is not so large as I expected, considering that a naval Battle was fought within it, which decided the fate of Sicily. It is not any way above two Miles, so that the Ships of the ancient Athenians and Syracusans must have been paltry Machines compared with those of the Moderns. The lesser Port which was so richly ornamented with Statues & surrounded by a Quay of Marbles, is now intirely filled up and ruined. It was built by Dionysius the elder, & was the Place, where the Ships of War and naval Stores of the Republic were kept. The Statues that surrounded it, as well as almost everything of the kind that was beautiful, were carried away by Verres.[107]

What was the Population of the ancient City is not easily determined, except one may be allowed to form a Conjecture from its extent. Strabo says that the Walls were twenty two miles in circumference,[108] but I am inclined to think this account exaggerated. The distance between Ortygia and Epipola is easily discover'd by the Latomiae, and was certainly not more than two miles. The extent the other way was not much more, as it never arrived to the Anapus, nor to the little Port of Trogilus, which are not more than three miles distant one from the other. The circumference of Syracuse must therefore have been nearly the same as that of Agrigentum and its Population in proportion.

May 23th we set out for Catania, leaving Augusta & Lentini, at which we were told that were [sic] nothing interesting. A few miles from Syracuse are the remains of an ancient fabric said to have been built by Marcellus, but I rather suppose it to be a tomb.

The Country of the Leontines formerly so celebrated for its fertility is now absolutely uninhabitable during the Summer from the badness of the Air. In several parts of it I observed the *triticum sylvestre*, or wild wheat, which grows spontaneously in the places, that are not cultivated. It is less than the common wheat and more difficult to separate from the Chaff, but its nutritive qualities are exactly the same. From this probably arose the fictions of Ceres, who is said to have first taught the culture of wheat in this Country.

The Plain of Catania is extremely rich but render'd desolate by the bad air. We crossed the Semetheus (now the Giaretta) which divides it, in a ferry, & soon perceived the tremendous ruins occasion'd by Mount Aetna.

[*Catania, May 23rd*][109]

In entering Catania one crosses the Lava of 1669, which appears still as fresh as the Year after the eruption. It broke out about twelve miles above the City, and poured down in a vast torrent, carrying inevitable destruction where ever it came. Instead of making Walls or trenches to avert its fury, the People of Catania, brought out St. Agatha's Veil, & a whole Legion of Saints, each of whom, the Priests assured them, was sufficient to perform much greater Miracles. The consequence of this was as usual. – A great part of the City was destroyed, its Port filled up and the Inhabitants ruined; but the Saints remained in greater credit than ever, the People readily believing that the Calamity arose from their own want of faith and not from any fault in their heavenly Guardians.

Soon after our arrival at Catania we waited upon the Prince of Biscari,[110] & had the pleasure for the first time of meeting with a noble subject of the King of Naples, whose acquaintance would be a valuable acquisition, in whatever station of life fortune had placed him.

The Appearance of his Feod at Biscari, the Affluence and Content of his Vassals, the affection with which they spoke of him, and the general Spirit of Improvement, that reigned thro' the whole gave me the most favorable Idea of him which was still encreased when I saw the order and economy of his family, & the Spirit and generosity, he shows in every thing, that can improve or adorn his Country. I can only lament, that the ungratefulness of the Soil renders the Labor and Skill of the Cultivator in a great measure fruitless. The natural jealous disposition of the Sicilians added to the bigotry and oppression of their Government, make them incapable of improvement. Whoever has Virtue or Spirit, to attempt it, only gains the reputation of a dangerous innovator, and meets with nothing but hatred and opposition from individuals and Persecution and suspicion from the Court.

We found the Prince in his Museum,[111] which is very rich and always open for the use of the Studious. In the first Apartment are the Marbles, among which are some excellent Busts and a torso of a Jupiter,[112] which appears to have been the true original of that, now in the *Museum Clementinum* at Rome. What remains is in perfect preservation and of the most exquisite Sculpture. There is a general majesty and repose thro' the whole, peculiar to the great Artists of Greece, when they attempted the Image of the Father of Gods and Men *omnia supercilio moventis*.[113] There are many other pieces of Sculpture in the Museum of great beauty and value, but when one has seen what is truly excellent, the Eye turns with indifference and even disgust to any thing of an inferior quality.

The Prince has besides a noble collection of Bronzes, Etruscan Vases, & natural curiosities and more particularly of Medals. His Sicilian ones are very numerous and well preserved & form an agreeable Study even to those, who are not versed in Antiquities. The taste and execution of the Greek Artists, is so superiorly fine, that their Medals consider'd merely as pieces of Sculpture are extremely interesting.

The Prince's Palace[114] is a great irregular building, the ancient part of it in the barbarous taste of the Sicilians, charged with monstrous figures, and unnatural ornaments, but the part, which he has built himself is simple, regular & elegant.

The City is almost intirely new, the Streets regular & spacious, but the houses built in a bad taste, and a great part of them only half-finished. The Churches are all in the modern Stile of Architecture, having been built since the year 1693, when the City was totally destroyed by an Earth-quake. Many of them, particularly the Cathedral, are extremely rich, but finished with Stones of different Colours, distorted into the most fantastick Shapes. One can scarce conceive any thing wild & monstrous, that is not to be found in the Buildings of modern Sicily. The Benedictine Convent is an immense fabric, built with vast expence, but in the usual Stile. It is not finished and probably never will be, as this City by reason of the nearness of Mount Aetna, can never hope for long duration. The Church is noble and magnificent. The inside of it was just completed, &, what is extraordinary, without any of the fashionable frippery; but they seem determined to make amends without for the little of the front that is finished, is not much inferior to the Palace of Prince Palagonia. It has a most excellent organ just finished. In the Convent is a good collection of Etruscan Vases, almost all as well as the Prince of Biscari's found in Sicily, a proof that this kind of Ware was not solely the manufacture of the Etruscans.

There is little else in Catania above Ground worthy of Notice. The Antiquities are all under the Lava. The Prince of Biscari has made great researches, and found a Theatre, Baths, Amphitheatre & some other buildings of less importance. The Theatre appears to have been very magnificent from the Columns, now imployed in the Cathedral. A Base and Pedestal of one of them, now stand in the Corte of the Prince of Biscari's Palace. They are of white Marble, very much charged with ornaments and appear to be of the Age of Trajan or the Antonines. The other antique Edifices have nothing particular, being only Masses of Brick and Stone, without any orders or ornaments, that I could distinguish.

The People of Catania, like the rest of the Sicilians, are extremely fond of attributing their antiquities to the Greeks, but without any reason, for the Greek City was totally destroyed by Sextus Pompeius.[115] It was soon after restored, but destroyed again by an eruption of Mount Aetna. By the assistance of the Romans it was rebuilt, & florished in great Splendor; till it was again overwhelmed by the same calamity. One cannot help wondering, that after such repeated destructions this City has been always rebuilt in the same Situation, a situation at the mouth of a Valley, which necessarily conducts the Lava down upon it. While there was a port for commerce, it is natural that the Love of gain should make people run great risks, but of late there has been no other motive, than the difficulty of changing Property, and even that seemed to be removed, when all was cover'd by burnt Rocks and turned into an uncultivable desert. The blind attachment to the Place of Nativity so natural to us all, and for which the subtilest Metaphysician cannot assign a reason, has vanquished every obstacle and Catania has been rebuilt after every destruction with more Splendor and magnificence than before. It now contains about 16 000. Inhabitants, who live in perpetual danger, but custom and implicit confidence in St. Agatha make them think little about it.

It has the privileges of being governed by its own Senate, & of never having a Garrison, hence it is daily increasing in wealth and magnificence, & the encouragement given by the Prince of Biscari to Art & Industry of every kind, gives it an appearance of life and activity, not to be observed in any other City of Sicily. He lately offer'd to build a Port which, if properly encouraged by the Court, would have render'd this City the great Emporium for the Commerce of this part of the Mediterranean, but unaccountable as it may seem, this offer met with opposition. The Prince has since imployed the money intended for this purpose in building an Aquaduct, which waters and renders fertile a vast extent of Country, and in covering with Soil and cultivating the Lava of 1669. He is also about publishing a large work upon the Antiquities of Catania, which from the Drawings I saw, promises much.

[Aetna, May 27th][116]

After having seen what was most worthy of attention in Catania we set out the 27th of May for the top of Mount Aetna.

As far as the Village of Nicolosi about 12. Miles, the ascent is gradual thro' rich Vineyards and fields planted with Mulberry-trees, except where the last torrents of Lava have destroyed them. The Sicilians call these places by a corrupted Spanish name Sciarra. That of 1669. broke out near Nicolosi, the neighbourhood of which is still cover'd with dry black Cinders, then thrown out. The Monticello with the Crater, from which the Lava flowed, are still bare, as if the eruption had been but yesterday, & will probably continue so for many ages, before the vicissitudes of weather have sufficiently moulder'd the burnt Matter, to render it capable of vegetation. I went to the top of it and saw round me immense numbers of the same kind, some almost bare, others richly planted with Vines, others cover'd with Groves of Oaks and others almost lost in succeeding floods of Lava which are also by the vast revolutions of ages mellowed into Soil and cloathed with Forests & Vineyards. A German Traveller[117] has said that this Monticello is as large as Vesuvius, but I walked to the top of it with ease in less than 10. minutes & I found the walk thro' the Cinders only of Vesuvius required at least two hours.

We reposed a little at the Convent of Nicolosi, and then pursued our journey attended by a Peasant of the Village call'd

Blasio, who usually serves as a Guide to those, who visit the Mountain. The *regione sylvosa* commences here and continues to the Cave called la *Grotta del Capro*, about 6. Miles. The ascent is all the way rapid & partly over the Lava of 1766. which must have made a most tremendous appearance, as it flowed four miles in breadth thro' a forest of Oaks. As we mounted higher, the ascent became very steep, and the change of climate very perceptible. At Catania they were in the midst of the Corn harvest, at Nicolosi every thing was in the bloom of May, but when we came near the Grotta del Capro, the trees were just putting their leaves and the Air felt extremely cold & piercing. We kindled a fire in this little Cave[118] and reposed ourselves till midnight, and then proceeded towards the Summet, thro' bare Cinders and fragments of Lava. After riding about eight miles, the Mountain became so steep, that we were obliged to quit our Mules and perform the remaining two miles on foot.

Here we stopped a while to contemplate the Scene before us. The Night was clear, and just light enough to show the general forms of the objects, but nothing distinct, – there was an universal Silence, except when interrupted at intervals by the Noise of the Mountain, which was loud & solemn, like the breaking of the Sea in a Storm. The Crater was distinguishable by a red gloomy light piercing thro' the vast volumes of Smoke, that rolled from it. – The whole together formed the most tremendous Scene I ever saw & which perhaps is not to be equalled any where else in the world.

We found very little Snow on this side of the Mountain, but the cold was so severe, that it was with the greatest difficulty, we could support it. Neither the weight of Cloaths, nor the labor of climbing through loose Cinders, which yielded to every step, could keep us warm. I had the misfortune to break my thermometre, and therefore cannot ascertain the exact degree of cold, but it was so intense, that the hot Vapor, which issued from the little cracks near the Crater, froze upon the Stones immediately.

After climbing about 2 hours with infinite labor and difficulty, we came to the edge of the Crater. The View, that here presented itself, is beyond all description or Imagination. The whole Island of Sicily, Malta, Calabria, & the Liparis appear just under one as in a map. The parts were all obscured in the blue tint of the morning and the whole together seemed wrapt in silence and repose. I felt myself elevated above humanity, & looked down with Contempt upon the mighty objects of Ambition under me. The Scenes where so many mighty Cities have florished in Art and Arms, where so many numerous fleets and Armies have fought for Universal Empire, seemed no more than a Spot,

E lui, ch'or Ocean chiamate, or Vasto,
Nulla equale a tui nomi ha in se di magno
Ma è bassa palude, & breve Stagno.
   Tasso[119]

As the Sun arose, the prospect gradually cleared, and the plains and Mountains, Lakes & Rivers, Cities and Forests became more and more distinct till they arrived to a certain pitch, and then vanished by the same degrees into the Vapors exhaled by the Sun. Aetna itself formed a vast Gnomon,[120] the Shade of which extended far beyond the visible horizon & convinced me that with a good Telescope both the Coasts of Africa and Apulia might be seen. I sometimes thought that, with a pocket-glass of Dolbands, I could distinguish the latter, but the cold was so intense, that I could not look with sufficient attention to be certain.

Plate 9 Charles Gore: *Temple, said to be of Juno Lacinia at Agrigentum*, 1777. Watercolour over pencil, 22.6 × 42.1 cm (Oo.4-31).

Plate 10 Charles Gore: *Temples, said to be of Juno and Concord, with a View of Agrigento in the Background*, 1777. Watercolour over pencil, 19.2 × 41.8 cm. Inscribed in brown ink: 'Temple of Juno Lucina –' (Oo.4-30).

Plate 11 (*opposite page*) Thomas Hearne: *Temple, said to be of Juno at Agrigentum*, 1777. Watercolour over pencil, 27.2 × 43.6 cm (Oo.4-29).

Plate 12 Charles Gore: *View of Syracuse from the Ruins of Olympeium, with the Remains of the Temple of Jupiter*, 1777. Watercolour over pencil, 18.8 × 37.3 cm. Inscribed in grey ink: 'Syracuse' (Oo.4-3).

Plate 13 Jacob Philipp Hackert: *Interior of the Cavern called the 'Ear of Dionysius' at Syracuse*, 1777. Pen and brown ink with brown wash over pencil, 44.4 × 33.8 cm. Inscribed in brown ink: 'L'oreille de/Dionise pres/de Siracuse/Ph. Hackert f./1777.' (Oo.4-33).

Plate 14 John Robert Cozens: *Mount Etna, from the Grotta del Capro*, 1777. Watercolour with scratching out over pencil, 35.8 × 48.4 cm (Oo.4-38).

Plate 15 Charles Gore and Thomas Hearne: *View of Mount Etna from the Convent of Nicolosi*, 1777. Watercolour with scratching out over pencil, 27.8 × 44.2 cm (Oo.4-39).

Plate 16 Jakob Philipp Hackert: *View of Mount Etna from Taormina*, 1777. Watercolour over pencil, 38.6 × 51.9 cm. Inscribed in grey ink: 'L'Etna prise à Toarmina.' and signed 'Ph. Hackert f. 1777.' (Oo.4-40).

Upon the Mountain under us we could trace the Streams of a vast number of Eruptions, which are yet nothing, compared to the number, which have been and which are no longer visible. The whole Mountain whose Base is near 100. Miles in circumference, and which, according to the observations of Mr. Canon Recupero[121] is near 5000. Yards perpendicular in height, has been thrown up; in examining into the deep vallees that have been worn by torrents, one sees that it is all composed of different Strata of Lava which have run one over another at long intervals of time being interlay'd with Soil of all depths from six Inches to ten feet, according to the time that elapsed between the eruptions. In the Lava that is most soft and easy to decay, it does not appear that a foot of Soil is produced in less than 1500 years, whence one may imagine, what numberless ages have been necessary to produce these vast operations of nature. But what must we think if a great part of this Mountain is only a reproduction, & that there has a higher summit fallen in, and been again thrown out. Of this, however, there is rather more than a probability, for about two thirds of the way up the third region, is a large plain, which extends unequally all round the Mountain, reaching in some places, particularly on the side towards Aci, almost down to the woods. Supposing the Mountain to have been originally of the conical form, usual and indeed necessary to Volcanos, all above this plain must have faln in. What now seems a basement to a smaller Mountain, must then have been continued in a gradual rise, to the top; so that Aetna was once considerably higher than at present. I wished to have examined with more leisure and attention into these wonders of Nature, but the cold, was so intense, that it was impossible to exist in it. I resolved however to look into the Crater before I descended.

Our Guide said much of the danger of it, and how often the banks fell in, but after a little persuasion and a number of prayers to St. Agatha, he led us to a place that had been already tried by some adventurous Stranger. From hence I looked into this tremendous Gulf of fire, and saw immense projecting rocks with vast volumes of Smoke, issuing from between them, mixed with a dim glimmering light. I could distinguish no bottom, but the tossing and beating of the Waves of melted Matter produced a Noise which gave me some Idea of the *floods & whirlwinds of tempestuous fire*[122] that rage beneath.

After having thus far gratified our curiosity, we returned almost frozen to the Cave, where we warmed and refreshed ourselves, and then proceeded towards Catania, where we arrived in the evening almost worn out with fatigue.[123]

(*Etna*. The height measured by Dr. Lind is only 10,954 feet, or 2 Miles, 131 Yards 10,700 feet English [?].

[?] in Peru is 15,833. feet geometrical, Snowdon 3,555 feet

Mont Blanc 15,662 feet

Vesuvius 3938. feet English

Teneriff 12,168 feet

Pinchincha 15,568 [?]

Gibraltar 1449.

Iron Gallery S.t Paul's 221.

Ben Nevis in Scotland 4372.

Chimboraso 20,608 feet.)

[*Aci Reale, June 1st*]

After reposing ourselves two days, we set out June 1st in the evening for Taormina, and lay at Aci reale.

The morrow morning we went a few miles out of the road, to see the famous Chesnut-trees, in which we were much disappointed. That called *la Castagna di cento Cavalli* is not a single tree, but a groupe, and the rest, tho' very large, are all Pollards very low and much mutilated. In Sicily they might be looked upon as wonders, as a great part of the Inhabitants never saw a tree larger than a Dwarf Olive, but to those who have been used to the noble Oaks of England, they are very contemptible objects.

I had however the consolation of seeing one of the most fertile and beautiful Countries in the World. Nothing can surpass the cultivated region of Mount Aetna, in the richness of Soil and luxuriance of vegetation, particularly the sides that have not lately suffer'd by eruptions. Almost every production of the Earth florishes in the utmost perfection, and the temperance and salubrity of the Air are equal to the fertility of the Soil. It is consequently exceedingly populous & consequently much better cultivated than any other part of Sicily. The number of the Inhabitants upon the whole Mountain is computed at 160 000. a much greater proportion than in any other part of the Island. On examining this side of the Mountain I was confirmed in my opinion, that it has once been higher, the chasm extended a great way down, and the edges of it are still very plainly to be distinguished.

[*Taormina, June 2nd*]

June 2nd we arrived at *Taormina*, anciently *Taurominium*. In our way we tasted the Waters of the *Acis*, so celebrated by the Poets. It is a cold limpid Stream, that flows from Mount Aetna and is now called *il fiume freddo*. A few miles beyond it is the *Oenobala*, now *la Cantara*, a considerable river, which bounds Mount Aetna to the North. Its channel is in some places worn very deep, and I observed that the bottom of it was a bed of Lava, but beyond I could find no appearance of Volcanic Matter.

At Taormina we were lodged by the Capuchins. The Town

21 The ruins of the Theatre at Taormina. Engraving after Jakob Philipp Hackert (British Library).

stands upon a high hill, immediately under which, on the south side, was the ancient City of Naxos, from whose ruins it sprung. It is at present poor & ill built, but its ruins sufficiently show its ancient Wealth and Magnificence. The principal of these is a Theatre[124] the best preserved that I have yet seen. It is of brick considerably larger and of a different construction from that of Aegesta. The outward Corridore is lost, but the Proscenium is almost intire, & one may still see the extent of the Scene, Podium etc. There are several Galleries and Chambers, the use of which Antiquarians cannot exactly determine, as they appear to have been too spacious and magnificent to have served merely for the Convenience of the Actors. The Theatre of Aegesta, which is of a much earlier date, than this, has nothing of the kind. It appears to have been no more than what was absolutely necessary for reciting and hearing the piece, but this appears to have been richly decorated and calculated for every kind of Show and pageantry, such as was in fashion under the Roman Emperors, when the purity of taste was corrupted. There are several mutilated Columns of Granite Cipoline & other costly Marbles lying about it, with Capitals and fragments of the Entablature of a corrupt Corinthian order, which prove the Theatre to have been built under the Romans, probably about the time of the Antonines. It is upon the side of a Hill, which commands a noble view of Mount Aetna and all the Coast of Sicily quite to Syracuse. Being detached from all modern buildings it has a very venerable appearance, which encreases when one reflects upon the Changes it has suffer'd – from being the place, where numerous & polite Audiences listened to the Works of Sophocles & Euripides,[125] to a refuge for Snakes, Lizzards etc. Besides the Theatre at Taormina, there are the foundations of a Temple, a Building supposed to have been a Naumachia,[126] and reservoirs of Water, but nothing very interesting. After spending a day there, we embarked upon a Maltese Speronara, which we had engaged at Catania, & in a few hours arrived at Messina.

[Messina][127]

As one enters the Faro,[128] the view is very beautiful and romantic, the Coasts being high and rocky, adorn'd with Towns & Villages, & gradually approaching each other. The entrance into the Harbour is still more striking – a beautiful Lake discloses itself gradually to the Eye, bounded on one side by a vast range of Houses, all uniform, which, tho' of bad Architecture, form a noble & magnificent Scene. Behind these rise the Heraean Mountains, cover'd with Woods & Vineyards, interspersed with Churches, Villas & Convents. On the other side a long Arm of land projects into the Sea, in the Shape of a Sickle, from which the City took its ancient name Zancle. Upon this are the Lighthouse, Lazzaretto & fortress, which is apparently built, not to defend the Town, but to command it.

Upon approaching nearer this fine Scene looses all its Splendor, and every object assumes an Air of melancholy and dejection. The Houses are many of them uninhabited, & the rest falling into ruin and decay. There were scarce any Vessels in the Port, and the Quay the most noble and extensive in the world, was only frequented by a few miserable fishermen. Every thing seemed to declare the fatal calamities that have lately overwhelmed this unfortunate City, and reduced it from the highest state of Wealth and felicity, to the lowest depth of misery and despair.

When we disembarked and enter'd the Town, the Prospect

still blackened – the Inhabitants were poor and ragged and the Houses, that seemed once to have been the residence of the great and Affluent, were cover'd with filth and falling into ruin. Of all the Cities in Europe perhaps none is more happily situated, than Messina. The Air is temperate & healthy, & the surrounding Country beautiful and fertile. Its port is large and convenient, & placed in the Centre of the Mediterranean, equally commodious for the eastern and western trade. These natural advantages were assisted by many privileges & immunities, granted by the Norman, German & Arragonian Kings.[129] As it was the first that opened its Gates to Ruggiero[130] who conquered the Island from the Sarazins, it seemed to have a right to particular favor & preeminence. So many happy circumstances naturally raised it to wealth & greatness. It contained 100 000. Inhabitants, and was the great Emporium for this part of the World; but as Wealth & Commerce naturally produce a love of Liberty, Messina grew tired of the Spanish Yoke & in 1672.[131] upon some provocation from the Viceroy, revolted. The Inhabitants defended themselves with great bravery & perseverance, & at last threw themselves under the protection of Lewis 14th. then at war with Spain, who after having been faithfully and effectually served by them, shamefully abandoned them in 1678. Ever since that time it has been the end of the Spanish Policy to distress and impoverish it. The Port is render'd almost useless by enormous charges, their Commerce is rigorously restrained, & every necessary of life heavily taxed. To add to these calamities, in 1743. the Plague swept away near three fourths of its inhabitants, which at present scarcely amount to 30 000.

We passed a few days in viewing the Town, but found nothing very interesting. The buildings are all of the modern Sicilian Stile, & except the Churches, falling into ruin. The Cathedral is a very moderate edifice, but has a tolerable Library, in which is a manuscript History of the revolt of 1672.[132] intitled: *Guere civili di Messina di Franc. Casiro Calabrese*. I read as much of it as the shortness of my time would permit, and wished much to have a Copy, but could by no means obtain it. It appears to be written in a very masterly manner, tho' the Stile is rather too close an imitation of Davila's.[133] It probably will never be suffered to appear in public, as the Spirit and impartiality, with which it is written, will be always displeasing to those in Power.

The Eddy of Caribdis, so tremendous in the description of the Poets,[134] is just without the Harbour of Messina. It never appears but when the wind blows against the Current, & then it has been known to swallow up small Vessels. In the time of Homer, when navigation was so little known, it was really terrible, and in that of Virgil not without danger, as the Romans were very contemptible Seamen, compared with the Moderns. The description of it in the Aeneid is very far beyond the reality even in the most tempestuous Weather:–

—Laevum implacata Charibdis
Obsidet, atque imo Barathri ter gurgite vastos
Sorbet in abruptum fluctus rursusque sub auras
Erigit alternos, et sidera verberat unda.
    Aen. 3[135]

I do not see however any reason for supposing that it was ever more violent than at present. Virgil writes as a Poet, not as a Naturalist, & the hyperbole is not stronger, than in many other parts of the same Poem.

After having thus far examined what is worthy of observation in Sicily, we embarked for Naples.[136]

I do not know whether so short a stay in the Island will justify my saying any thing of the general Character of its Inhabitants. In most other Countries, it is what I should not venture at, till after long experience and mature observation, but here the features are so strong, that it is difficult to miss a resemblance.

We found the Sicilians in general very different in their Customs & manners from those of the Capital. The Nobility & Courtiers of most of the Nations of Europe are nearly the same. A Constant intercourse with each other has worn away all the characteristic touches of Nature, and left nothing but a kind of negligent Civility, expressed with great volubility of words but signifying nothing. Even this is render'd disgusting in most Countries by affectation & fashion, which have made the People of Birth & fortune a more or less awkward imitation of the French. It is remote from Courts & great Cities that one must search for national Characters. There one finds the Sicilians jealous & passionate, & like most of the Inhabitants of warm Climates, averse to labor and prone to pleasure, & superstition. They are hospitable and kind to Strangers, and as far as I am able to judge, fair and honest in their dealings. They are extremely ignorant & superstition prevails among them to an incredible degree, even among People, whose rank and condition in life ought to place them above it. I observed at a Ball in Catania several Noblemen of distinction, dressed in a kind of Livery of red and blue. Upon asking the reason of this singularity, I was informed that it was a vow made to St. Agatha during sickness to wear nothing, but her Livery for a certain time.

The Ecclesiastiks are immensely numerous & possess above one third of the Island, which being totally exempt from Taxes, the rest is of course heavily burdened. However the bigotry of the Sicilians is such, that an attempt to tax them, would be unpopular, as the reduction of their number has been found to be. Their influence is so great, that all inquiry or improvement of every kind is checked. Men, who gain vast emoluments of the blind belief of a few incomprehensible Mysteries, are naturally very jealous of every thing, that can tend to dissipate the cloud of darkness, which protects them. Weak as human reason is, it would be sufficient in its lowest state to penetrate the thin veil of Priestcraft, if People only dared think; but the greatest Part of Mankind believe because they have never had the Courage to ask their own understandings, whether they believe or not.

The Ecclesiasticks in Sicily, as well as every where else, are perfectly sensible of this, & therefore oppose every thing, that can possibly imploy the mind. The trifling Indiscretion of a British Traveller, in publishing part of a private conversation had like to have ruined the learned Canon Recupero of Catania,[137] & will probably prevent his valuable Work upon Mount Aetna from ever appearing to the World. The Bishop gave him a very severe admonition, & an absolute injunction, not to mention any thing for the future, that could possibly invalidate the Authority of Moses. Thus is a Man of real learning & Genius render'd useless to the World, & those Parts & accomplishments, which ought to raise him to honor and Affluence, only expose him to danger & persecution.

This fear of innovation keeps the Sicilians in a State of the most profound ignorance. Arts & Sciences of every kind are despised & unknown, & even the common implements of husbandry are in a very imperfect state. Their Corn is trod out by Oxen, and ground by Hand, there not being a single flour Mill in the whole Island. There was a Windmill lately built at Girgenti, but the prejudices of the People were such, that they would not use the flour, so it was pulled down.

Before the time of Victor Amadeus,[138] they scarcely knew how to make butter & cheese, and were equally ignorant in the culture of their Vines. That active and enterprizing Prince not only improved their domestic Economy but introduced the Arts of Peace & good Government, as far as the shortness of his reign would permit. Before his time, every Nobleman was a petty Tyrant and kept a band of Cut-throats in his pay, who committed every kind of disorder. The Country was likewise so infested with Robbers that all communication by Land was cut off. He made every Nobleman answerable for the conduct of his Domestics, and all damages sustained by robbers, between the rising & setting of the Sun, recoverable from the Community of the district, in which the offence was committed.

Since these salutary Laws, justice has been much better administer'd, & Robberies & murders less frequent in Sicily, than in the Southern parts of Italy. In the prisons of Girgenti there were above 70. People and only one for murder. In the Hospital there was not a single Patient, that had been stabbed, while in the Kingdom of Naples, every Hospital and Infirmary is full of them. The Stories that have been published about Bands of Robbers confederated throughout the Island, & under the protection of Government, are intirely without foundation. The Robbers in Sicily as well as in England are generally Individuals of desperate Fortunes who seldom murder except resisted for according to the Laws murder is rigorously punished with Death but a simple Robbery not attended by any atrocious circumstances, with the Gallies.

It is true that favor & protection occasion these Laws being often very partially executed tho' perhaps less so than at Naples. An active & just Magistracy would render Sicily one of the happiest Countries in the world, as the Code of Laws of the Emperor Frederick the 2nd [139] is still in force & is one of the wisest, that ever was composed; But the dispensing Power of the King ruins all. This being delegated to the Viceroy, & from him to his Officers, Dependents etc. is in the end sold to the highest bidder; thus great Criminals escape with impunity, while little ones suffer.

What gave HVB such tremendous Notions of the Sicilian Robbers was probably a custom of the Noblemen of never travelling without a long train of armed Followers; but these are their Tenants & Vassals, who keep up the ancient feodal custom of accompanying, in his expeditions, their Landlord, more to make a show of his wealth and power than for defence.[140]

The accounts that we have had of the Climate, are equally remote from truth. The Air is thin, dry & clear, & tho' the heats in the middle of the day are frequently excessive, the Mornings & Evenings are always refreshed with a Breeze from the Sea or the Mountains. We had the Siroc Winds very frequently during our journey, but the heat never surpassed what I have known in sultry days in England. I enquired of every Body whose observation & experience I could rely upon, & all agreed, that the Thermometre never rose so high, even in the hottest Months, as we have been taught to believe.

There seems to be a kind of pleasure natural to Man in telling as well as hearing Wonders. It flatters our pride by giving us imaginary superiority, which is equally grateful, as if it was real. To instruct or inform others suppose that we are possest of some knowledge, which they want, & the more wonderful & extraordinary this is the more our own superiority is enhanced, & the more the mind of the hearer is imployed. A relation of the occurrences of common life, & even the Histories of wise Legislators and just Magistrates are read with coldness and indifference, tho' their examples afford the most salutary & useful lessons for the Conduct of all; but we attend with pleasure to the mad actions of Heroes & Conquerors, tho' they can be of no possible use to us.[141]

Men are always amused when their passions are interested, & Imaginations roused, & we are naturally inclined to believe whatever amuses us. Hence the number of improbable fables, that have been so tenaciously supported & industriously spread. When once we have determined to believe a thing, its very absurdity confirms it. We persist because we are ashamed to own that we could have been so grossly mistaken. Happy had it been for the world if this principle had extended no further than to amuse the Idle & inquisitive, & not maintained itself, as it has too often, by every species of cruelty and oppression. It is this fatal credulity, that has laid waste the most delightful regions of the Earth, & driven Science & pleasure into the rude and inclement Climates of the North. It would have followed even there, but the natural want of necessaries to sustain life called forth industry and ingenuity to its aid. The Mind being thus put in motion, & the Understanding obliged from physical Necessity to act, followed the natural course of reason, which soon discover'd how vain and impotent was the Phantasm, which had been revered with so much awe. Thus from physical evil comes moral good.

In looking over Sicily, one is likewise tempted to draw another conclusion & to think, that moral evil springs from physical good. The fertility of the Soil and temperature of the Air supplying every natural want of the Inhabitants, their mental faculties are never call'd into & one generation succeeds another *ut unde supervenit undam*.[142] In examining the History of the Greek republics, this truth is still more plain. While divided into a number of little states, confined to a portion of land too small to support the Citizens, exposed to foreign invasion & perpetually at variance among themselves, their artificial wants supplied the place of natural ones, & obliged them all to be active & attentive. Arts, sciences and commerce florished, & the Spirit of emulation mutually transfer'd itself from Individuals to Societies and from Societies to Individuals; but when they were all subjected to one Power, they became secure and indolent.[143] The fear of worse and hopes of better, those general Springs of human Actions, ceased; & Sicily in spite of all its advantages, sunk into Barbarism & ignorance, which, when once established, support themselves.

Bad however as the present State of Sicily is, it would soon recover, if the restrictions imposed by Government, were removed. Ease and pleasure would introduce foreign luxury & create artificial wants. To gratify these, Industry and ingenuity would be called forth, Manufactures would be established, and every means of gain put in practice. When ease & pleasure are to be procured by Wealth, every individual is desirous of acquiring it, and when human Genius is left at Liberty, the means are easily found. Sicily is besides formed by Nature for Commerce, situated in the Centre of the Mediterranean, furnished with excellent Ports, capable of containing fleets of any number, but the narrow Politicks of Spain have subjected almost every article of commerce to severe restrictions & burdensome taxes. Manufacturies of every kind are discouraged, lest wealth should raise a Spirit of Liberty, as it did in Messina in 1672. The whole Levant trade, which Sicily might almost engross, is absolutely prohibited since the Plague of Messina, not so much from the caution of Government, as from the bigotry of the Priests, who attribute that Calamity to the judgment of Heaven upon the Messenese for connecting themselves too intimately with Infidels.

The articles of trade in Sicily are innumerable. There is scarce any production of the Earth, which some part or other of the Island does not favor. The riches under ground are not less abundant than those above, the Hills being full of rich Mines of various Metals, and inexhaustable quarries of the most costly Marbles.

The Genius of the Sicilians seems also much more adapted to commerce, than that of the southern Italians, being more lively, free & enterprizing. Their Manner of living, except in the Capital, is disagreeable, as the Women mix very little in Company. Even those of the first rank seldom dine or sup with any but their own family. Having so little intercourse with the World, they are extremely ignorant and impolished. A Monastic education disposes them much to Devotion, which generally ends in the most rigid bigotry, or abandoned debauchery, according as their beauty or temperament exposes them to temptation. As they have no other principles of conduct, but what they bring from a Convent they are very open to seduction. Conscious of this their Husbands are very attentive in guarding them, but in these cases force & Vigilance seldom succeed. *Ut ameris amabilis esto*![144] is the only lesson that can ensure conjugal felicity, & ought equally to be attended to by both Sexes.

However opposite the principles of Christianity may seem to a life of pleasure and dissipation, experience shows, that, even when most seriously believed, they rather assist the gratifications of the Passions. The same amiable weakness, that leads to Love, leads to superstition, & the flattering doctrine of repentance easily reconciles them. Even the principles of the most reasonable Believers are built upon slippery foundations, & if they cannot be accommodated to the inclinations of the Heart, are easily overturned by the magic of the tongue. Religion is a very deceiving weapon in defence of Virtue, which often encourages to resist, when the only way of safety lay in flight. It gives confidence without force, & dazzles without enlightening. Women are seldom taught to think, – their Notions are received without having been examined, and are therefore easily confuted. The prejudices of education, however deeply engrafted, are but feeble arms against eloquence aided by sentiment. Is a mind unused to reason almost any thing may be persuaded, when urged in proper time; and so disguised as not to shock any preestablished Notions of delicacy and decorum.

Knowledge is the only effectual Guard of Virtue. Opinions that have been attentively examined on every side are slowly adopted but, when once fixed, difficult to be removed. Those who are taught to consider the Nature and bounds of Moral right & wrong, and to know their real situation in Life, have no further wish, than to act well the part alotted to them in Society. They see how great a Share of necessary pain is mixed with all human Pleasures, & that the surest means of living happy is to conform as much as possible to the Laws & Customs under which fortune has placed them. They will find, that those Laws, though different from their Ideas of perfection, were instituted for the general Good, and that who ever transgresses them, forfeits their protection, by which much more is lost than can possibly be gained by any transitory pleasure. The favorite Maxim of a Monastic Education, that young People ought to obey the instructions of their Tutors, & not to reason upon them, delivers them over at once to the guidance of Passion. It founds the Principle of Duty upon fear, & when this or any other Passion becomes the rule of conduct, the transition to an other is very easy. Love or vanity soon take its place and then there is no need of seduction.[145]

This is the only education of the Sicilian Ladies, & the consequences are such as may reasonably be expected. At the moment of their marriage they either plunge into every excess of dissipation & debauchery or are deprived by the jealousy of their husbands of every amiable & elegant enjoyment of Society. It is true that in warm climates People are generally more given to pleasures than in cold ones, but this natural disposition is never so strong, but it may be corrected by salutary institutions, as may be seen in the Histories of the early Greeks and Romans.

The Sicilians like the Neapolitans are extremely fond of every thing that is gaudy & glittering, – their dress is generally fine and dirty. The furniture of their Houses, their public and private buildings are all in the same stile. They ever affect strong oppositions of colours and unnatural phantastic forms. This love of false brilliancy, from which none of the moderns are totally free, has been attributed by the Northern Nations to the heat of climate, & this Opinion having been supported by Montesquieu[146] has become rather general. But the climate of Sicily was the same anciently as at present, tho' the national Character is totally changed.

The Sicilian Greeks were remarkable above all others for the elegance & refinement of their pleasures, & all the monuments of their taste, that are come down to us are distinguished by an excess of purity & simplicity, & if they have any fault it is in too great a neglect of minute ornaments. If therefore we attribute this change to physical causes, we must suppose, that there has been some great Alteration in the organization of the Inhabitants, which could only have been produced by a total change of food & manner of living, or by some general epidemic disease. The differences of the first are but trifling, & there has no new disease appeared sufficiently powerful, except that dreadful one, which pollutes generation in its source, & which for some time threatened the destruction of the human Race. The disorders, which that has produced in weakening the Constitutions, & deranging the nerves are certainly very great; but as a wild & extravagant taste appear'd in Europe before that was known, we must attribute it to some other causes.

Perhaps one of the most powerful is that love of novelty so natural to us all. To imitate others is to acknowledge their superiority, & that is what our pride will not suffer us to do. Hence human Affairs are in a perpetual State of fluctuation. They rise gradually to the utmost perfection, that they are capable of, & then by endeavoring to surpass it, run into affectation & extravagance. This variation is observable in all the fine Arts, but more particularly in Sculpture, and Architecture, which depending intirely upon form, their beauties are more limited. The space of perfection is very narrow between negligence & affectation, & we easily run into rudeness on one side, or excess of refinement on the other.

An other cause of the superiority of the Ancients in works of taste was their Religion. The elegant Mythology of the Greeks & Romans, whose Deities were moral and Physical Virtues personified, afforded every possible advantage to art. Wisdom, Virtue, Majesty, Strength & Agility were all represented under the persons of different divinities. The Artist was confined to a particular character, which his aim was to render as perfect as possible. He had not only all Nature before him to choose what was best in its kind, but the experience of all those, who had gone before him in the same way. He could bewilder himself in vain researches after novelty, for his subject was limited & he had no other way of gratifying that love of distinction, natural to all, but by really excelling. A Statue or picture was then the affair of a Nation, as they naturally supposed that the Gods would be most propitious to those who gave them the best. Hence Artists became Characters of importance in the State, & were generally Men of Birth and Education, the Friends and Companions, not the Servants & dependents of Kings & Ministers. It was not thought sufficient, that they should be thoroughly instructed in the mechanic Parts of their Profession, but they were deeply read in History, Poetry and Philosophy. Their Imaginations were thus elevated and corrected, and their Works were the produce of long Study as well as accurate execution. When those noble Master-pieces were placed in the Temples, the People at large had an opportunity of examining their beauties & their eyes became accustomed to elegant & simple forms. Hence good taste became general. – Poets, Orators, Painters, Sculptors & Architects were all animated by the same Spirit, & the People from the highest to the lowest were all capable of judging of their Merit. The same taste extended to every thing, & dress, Household-furniture, & even Kitchen Utensils were distinguished by a purity and elegance of design.

But the sour Mythology of the Christians changed all. Beauty & elegance of every kind were not only despised, but any attention to them condemned as impious & profane. The Temples were demolished & the Statues broken in pieces by these fierce Enthusiasts, & the most barbarous Structures & figures substituted in their places. Even when Commerce & Liberty began to restore the Arts in Italy, the Subjects which Religion allowed for painting & Sculpture were so bad, that it was impossible for them, to approach their ancient perfection. The lives & sufferings of Saints, whose characteristics were abject submission & humility, degraded Art & Genius. Instead of endeavoring to exalt Nature, they were obliged to abase her, & out of respect to superstition, to load their figures with heavy draperies, which they endeavored to vary by a diversity of colours & forms; hence they ran into that unnatural extravagance which prevails more or less in almost all their works.

Another cause of the decline of taste, might be the corruption of Languages; for as words are the signs of Ideas, & the principal means by which we abstract and compound them, a want of precision in one produces a want of precision in an other. – Thus languages have a very considerable influence upon National Characters. When the Roman Empire was falling to ruin and the Soldiers had trampled upon the Laws & reduced the Government to a kind of military Oligarchy, Adventurers of all Nations were raised by them to the supreme Power. These being illiterate Barbarians totally destroyed the purity of the Latin tongue, which tyranny and oppression had long before impaired. This evil was soon after encreased, when the rude & warlike Nations of the North overran the Empire & mixed their own barbarous Jargon with the noble & expressive Languages of the Ancients.

A general confusion of terms ensued, & tho' the modern dialects that have sprung from the ruins are better than could have been expected, they never can arrive at the force, majesty & precision of the Greek & Latin.

Such appear to me to have been the causes of the ruin of taste. A number of accidental circumstances have contributed to make them more prevalent in one Country, than another. In Sicily I believe it is much worse than in any other part of Europe, excepting only some States of Germany. To determine how far it is ever likely to return to its ancient purity would lead me into too long a dissertation at present, but I am inclined to believe, that nothing less than another general Revolution in Europe could effect it, and that does not seem likely to happen.[147]

Notes on the 'Expedition into Sicily'

For full details of abbreviated references, see Bibliographical Note, page 20.

1 Claude Gellée, called Le Lorrain (1600–82), whose paintings were popular with English collectors throughout the eighteenth century. Knight had a particular predilection for this artist. He owned a painting by him, as well as more than 250 drawings which he bequeathed to the British Museum, see *Arrogant Connoisseur*, 99–100, and M. Roethlisberger, *Claude Lorrain, the Drawings* (London 1968), I, 453. The architecture of Knight's house at Downton in Herefordshire was inspired by a painting by Claude, *La Crescenza*, now in the Metropolitan Museum of Art, New York, which was in Knight's possession at the time of construction, see *Arrogant Connoisseur*, 40–41, M. Kitson, *Claude Lorraine – Liber Veritatis* (London 1978), 126–7, and S. Lang, 'Richard Payne Knight and the Idea of Modernity', in J. Summerson (ed.), *Concerning Architecture: Essays on Architectural Writers presented to Nikolaus Pevsner* (London 1968), 86.

2 The Greek colony of Paestum, or Poseidonia, passed to Rome in 273 BC. It declined towards the end of the Empire because of malaria, which finally drove out its inhabitants. For the most comprehensive account of the history of the site, see A. F. Pauly and G. Wissowa, *Real-Encyclopädie der Classischen Altertumswissenschaften* (Stuttgart 1893–1972), XXXXIII, *Nachträge*: Poseidonia. It comprises three major Doric temples, which in the eighteenth century were called – from north to south – the Basilica, the Temple of Poseidon and the Temple of Ceres. For modern nomenclature and archaeological studies on the temples, see F. Krauss, *Paestum, die griechischen Tempel* (Berlin 1978), 4th ed., with all relevant earlier literature. Unlike Herculaneum or Pompeii, the temples at Paestum had never been submerged, but because of their comparative isolation simply remained unnoticed until 1746. Once rediscovered, the temples became the most popular and accessible site for the study of Greek architecture outside Greece.

3 Publius Vergilius Maro, poet (70–19 BC). His major works are the *Eclogues*, a loose collection of poems mixing Greek with Italian elements and an idealised Arcadia with contemporary history; the *Georgics*, which deal with country life, the cultivation of crops, fruit trees, etc. (from which Knight also quotes), and the *Aeneid*, the story of Aeneas, the legendary founder of Rome. The quotation here is taken from the *Georgics*, III, 146. It is translated in the Loeb edition (see Bibliographical Note p. 20): 'Round the groves of Silarus and the green holm-oaks of Alburnus swarms a fly . . . .' An early edition of Virgil's *Georgics* can be found in the *Sales Catalogue*, lot 743: 'Virgili Opera, Burmanni 1746'. Precisely the same quotation from Virgil to describe the same phenomenon was used by J. Berkenhout, *The Ruins of Poestum or Poseidonia, . . .* (London 1767), I, n. 6, which Knight may well have known.

4 Virgil, *Georgics*, III, 151.

5 The building material used for most of the architecture at Paestum is travertine, a soft local limestone. On the use of cement and mortar at Paestum and elsewhere and respective references in ancient literature, see M. E. Blake, *Ancient Roman Construction in Italy from the Prehistoric Period to Augustus* (Washington 1947), 308–52.

6 Knight's assessment of the architecture of Paestum is extraordinarily perceptive compared with other travellers' views, see for instance *Arrogant Connoisseur*, 21 and 79. Even Goethe, who visited the site ten years later, had to make a conscious effort – reminding himself of the 'rules of art history' – to appreciate the massive Doric temples: Goethe, *Italienische Reise*, 'Hamburg-edition' (Munich 1978), XI, 219–20.

7 Augustus (emperor 27 BC–AD 14) and the Antonines: Antoninus Pius (emperor AD 137–61), Marcus Aurelius (emperor AD 161–80) and Lucius Verus (emperor AD 161–9). Contrary to later views, Knight and many of his contemporaries admired Roman art and architecture of the later Empire, see *Arrogant Connoisseur*, 78.

8 Knight's discussion of the Corinthian order at Paestum and elsewhere is confusing and confused. His source for the legend concerning the invention of the Corinthian order is obviously Vitruvius, *On Architecture* (ed. Loeb, 2 vols, London/New York 1931–4), IV, C, I, 9. Whence he derived his information about the origins of the Corinthian order, however, and how he came to the conclusion that the columns and capitals were Corinthian but the entablature Doric, is obscure. None of the standard books of the day on architecture, all of which are listed in the *Sales Catalogue* and which Knight may well have used for his researches, hold this view: Sir William Chambers, *Treatise on Civil Architecture* (London 1759); A. Desgotez, *Les Edifices de Rome* (Paris 1682); James Gibbs, *A Book of Architecture* (London 1728). Not even a more specialised work on Paestum – also in the *Sales Catalogue* – mentions this feature: A. S. Mazochi, 'Commentatorium', in *Aeneas Tabules Heracleenses* (Naples 1754), 498. If Knight reached his mistaken opinion independently, he may have been misled by the unusual mixture of provincial South Italian, Ionic and barbaric elements of the capitals at Paestum, which are nevertheless Doric.

9 Strabo (c.64 BC–c.AD 21), geographer and historian, whose work, after that of Ptolemy, is the main source for ancient geography. He mentions Paestum in his *Geography* (see Bibliographical Note, p. 20), V, 4, 13, as rendered unhealthy by a nearby river. Lots 535 and 796 in the *Sales Catalogue* are editions of Strabo's work.

10 In his assessment of the late Empire as a period of decline, Knight shows himself well aware of contemporary historical theory. With the works of Montesquieu (see n. 146 below) – which Knight was acquainted with – and others, the idea of a cyclical development of history, which could be exemplified in the rise and decline of the Roman Empire, had become popular among historians and writers on art and architecture. See A. Momigliano, 'Ancient History and the Antiquarian', *Journal of the Warburg and Courtauld Institutes*, XIII (1950), 285 ff., and A. Momigliano, 'Eighteenth-century prelude to Mr Gibbon', in *Gibbon et Rome à la lumière de l'Historiographie Moderne* (Geneva 1977).

11 For the story of Palinurus, Aeneas' helmsman, see *Aeneid*, V, 833–70: 'Overcome by sleep, he fell overboard, was washed up on the shore of Italy and there murdered by the Lucanians.'

12 Horace, *Satires*, ed. Loeb (London/New York 1926), II, VI, 61. I am indebted to Brian Cook for the source of this quotation.

13 This cave is still known today as the Grotta delle Ossa, about four miles east of Capo Palinuro. Its walls are covered with incrustations of human and animal bones, which for a long time were thought to be the remains of victims of two major shipwrecks known to have occurred in this area during the Roman period. More recent studies have revealed the remains of antediluvian animals and flintstone weapons.

14 Two views of Stromboli by Charles Gore are preserved in the British Museum (Payne Knight Bequest, Oo.4-5, 6; Pls 1 and 2). Both are inscribed and dated by J. Ph. Hackert, presumably to record their place in the context of Knight's diary, see *Arrogant Connoisseur*, 151, no. 98. Twelve related sketches by Gore in the Goethe-Nationalmuseum, Weimar (Th. Scr. 2.2³–13) show how carefully prepared the final versions of the watercolours were.

15 Thomas Fazellus (1498–1570), first modern historian of Sicily, wrote *De Rebus Siculis* (Palermo 1558), which was republished several times during the eighteenth century. The edition referred to below is by J. Graevius and P. Burmannus in the *Thesaurus Antiquitatum Historiarum nobilissarium Insularum Siciliae, Sardiniae . . .* (Leiden 1723–5), X, IV. A copy of this edition is in the *Sales Catalogue*, lot 627. Fazellus' comments on Volcano are on p. 4C. On Fazellus' writings, see A. Momigliano, n. 10 above, 'Ancient History and the Antiquarian'.

16 Paulus Orosius, *Historiae adversum Paganos*, transl. I. W. Raymond (New York 1936), IV, 20, 30. Orosius, a Spaniard, is known to have fled from the Vandals to Africa in AD 414. He became a pupil of St Augustine and wrote a history of the world in seven books, which were still widely read in the eighteenth century. Knight's criticism of Fazellus is, indeed, correct. Both Thucydides (see n. 17) and Aristotle (see n. 18) confirm the earlier date for the creation of Volcano. Knight's suggestion that Orosius was the source for Fazellus' error shows how very carefully he must have read and compared these texts.

17 Thucydides (*c.*460–*c.*400 BC), Athenian general, author of the (incomplete) *History of the Peloponnesian War* in eight books. The reference to Volcano, i.e. Hiera, is in ed. Loeb (4 vols, London/New York 1919–23), III, LXXXVIII. Lot 803 in the *Sales Catalogue* is 'Thucydides, Graecum Scholiis, Junta 1506'.

18 Aristotle (384–322 BC) mentions Volcano (see n. 16), which he calls by its Greek name, 'Hiera', in his *Meteorologica*, ed. Loeb (London/Cambridge, Mass. 1952), II, VIII, 211.

19 Originally probably the god of volcanic phenomena and destructive fire in general, Vulcan was in Classical times identified with Hephaestus, the god of smiths.

20 Strabo (see n. 9 above), *Geography*, VI, 2, 10.

21 Cicero (106–43 BC), *The Verrine Orations* (see Bibliographical Note, p. 20), II, III, 37. For details see n. 30 below.

22 Aeolus, the ruler of the winds, is said by Homer, *Odyssey*, ed. Loeb (2 vols, London/New York 1919), X, 1–2, to live in Aeolia, a floating island, where according to Virgil, *Aeneid*, I, 52–9, he keeps the winds in a cave.

23 Virgil, *Aeneid*, I, 56: 'In his lofty citadel sits Aeolus . . . .'

24 Ibid., 55–6: 'They, to the mountain's mighty moans, chafe blustering around the barriers.'

25 Gaius Valerius Flaccus began his only known poem, the *Argonautica*, in about AD 80. The quotation here is translated in the Loeb edition (London/Cambridge, Mass. 1934), I, 579–82, as: 'There stands in the Sicilian sea on the side of the retreating Pelorum a crag, the terror of the straits, high as are the piles it lifts into the air, even so deep are those that sink below the surface of the waters . . . .' An edition of the *Argonautica* is in the *Sales Catalogue*, lot 548.

26 Pliny the Elder (AD 23/4–79), Roman historian, of whose works only the *Natural History* survives. The passage referred to is ed. Loeb (10 vols, London/Cambridge, Mass. 1938–62), III, IX.

27 Strabo (see n. 9 above), *Geography*, II, 5, 19.

28 See n. 22 above.

29 Tindari, the ancient Tyndaris, was a flourishing Roman commercial and cultural centre until its destruction (whether by earthquake, landslide or military force is uncertain). The theatre dates from the fourth century BC, when Tyndaris was founded. The 'temple' or basilica is a Roman building of the first century BC.

30 Gaius Verres, as quaestor and legate, plundered the provinces under his administration and flagrantly abused his position. As proconsul in Sicily (73–71 BC), he exploited and oppressed the province by force and chicanery. Cicero, representing the Sicilians, successfully launched a prosecution against him and secured his condemnation for extortion. Cicero published some of his orations against Verres, from which Knight quotes frequently.

Knight's detailed knowledge of these events was presumably derived not only from Cicero's writings but also from the surprisingly large number of contemporary comments on the issue. The Abbé Fraguier, in his dissertation *On the Gallery of Verres*, published by G. Turnbull in 1740, and C. Middleton's account of Verres' confiscation of works of art, in *History of the Life of Cicero* (London 1741), II, 79–111, condemn Verres' plundering of the Sicilian cities, as does Knight. C. Cameron in *The Baths of the Romans* (London 1772), 3–8, and later J. Dallaway in *Of Statuary* (London 1816), 135 ff., however, defend the general principle of looting works of art. They argue that as a result of exhibiting the statues in public places in Rome, the Romans' taste improved greatly. The issue must have been of interest as a historical precedent for contemporary English collectors in their passion for buying works of art when abroad and displaying them in their country houses. The most recent study of Verres is F. H. Cowles, 'Gaius Verres: an historical study', in *Cornell Studies of Classical Philology*, XX (1917). Knight's reference here is to a specific incident, related by Cicero in *The Verrine Orations*, II, IV, 39–40: Verres had ordered a revered statue of Hermes to be taken from Tyndaris, where it stood in a temple. The local senate refused and Verres, to enforce his demand, had the head of the senate stripped and exposed in the market-place until the statue was delivered.

31 This incident confirms the impression given by Goethe (*Gedenkausgabe der Werke, Briefe und Gespräche*, ed. E. Beutler [Zurich 1965], XIII, 594 ff.) that Hackert was, if not the most senior, certainly the most influential member of the party, who knew how to use his connections with the court at Naples. He must have received his letters of recommendation through distinguished friends at the capital of the Two Sicilies, where he was later to become court painter, see B. Lohse, *Jakob Philipp Hackert, Leben und Anfänge seiner Kunst* (Emsdetten 1936), 23–4. A detailed study by W. Krönig of Hackert's views of Sicily is to be published in 1986.

32 Diodorus Siculus, from Agyrion in Sicily, flourished under Caesar and Augustus (to at least 21 BC). He wrote (c.60–30 BC) a world history in forty books (see Bibliographical Note, p. 20), which is one of the most important sources for the early history of Sicily. On the Heraean Mountains see IV, 84 (1–2). An edition of this work is also recorded in the *Sales Catalogue*, lot 643.

33 Halontion, today S. Marco di Alunzio, is mentioned by Cicero in *The Verrine Orations*, II, III, 43, 103; II, IV, 23, 51.

34 Cefalù, the ancient Kephaloidion. A watercolour of a 'View of Cephalu' by Thomas Hearne is in the Payne Knight Bequest (British Museum, Oo.4-41; fig. 13).

35 Fazellus, op. cit. (n. 15 above), 241 AC.

36 Himera was founded by Greek settlers in the seventh century BC, the first colony to be established on the north coast of Sicily. The Ionic-Chalcidian culture of Himera was subverted in 476 BC by Theron of Acragas (see n. 71, 80) who, to avenge his son Thrasideos, exterminated the Ionic inhabitants of the city and replaced them with Doric colonists. (This is presumably what Knight is referring to when he mistakenly speaks of Hannibal's revenge for his grandfather as the motive for the destruction of Himera, see n. 66.) In 480 BC Himera was the site of a famous battle between a league of Sicilian Greeks under Theron of Acragas and Gelon of Syracuse (see n. 93) on one side and the Carthaginians under Hamilcar on the other. (This was Hamilcar Barca, a fifth-century Carthaginian general, not Hannibal's father, who lived 200 years later, nor even Hannibal himself, as Knight suggests.) The overwhelming Greek victory resulted in the rout of the Carthaginian army and destruction of their fleet. For seventy years this victory put a stop to the territorial ambitions of Carthage, until 409 BC when the Carthaginians returned to attack the Doric cities of Sicily. Himera was razed to the ground and abandoned. Knight was certainly less accurate in his reading of the sources here than elsewhere.

37 Thucydides (see n. 17), *History*, ed. Loeb (4 vols, London/New York 1919–23), VI, v.

38 See n. 36 for Knight's factual errors.

39 P. C. Scipio Aemilianus Africanus Numatinus (185/4–129 BC), Roman general, who achieved great distinction in the Third Punic War, which ended with his destruction of Carthage in 146 BC. A man of strict personal morality, courageous, cultured and intellectual, he returned to their rightful owners works of art taken from Sicily by the Carthaginians after previous victories. See Cicero, *The Verrine Orations*, II, IV, 33, 73.

40 Stesichorus, lyric poet, said to have lived at Himera in the first half of the sixth century BC.

41 For Verres and his art robberies, see n. 30.

42 La Bagaria or Villa Palagonia, built in 1715 by Tommaso Napoli for Ferdinando Francesco II, Prince of Palagonia. The bizarre architecture – see K. Lohmeyer, *Palagonisches Barock* (Berlin 1942) and A. Blunt, *Sicilian Baroque* (London 1968) – was criticised in a similar way also by other travellers, see H. Tuzet, *La Sicile au XVIIIe siècle vue par les voyageurs étrangers* (Strasbourg 1955), 288–9.

43 Palermo, formerly Panormos, the capital of Sicily, founded by the Phoenicians, remained the centre of Punic settlement until its conquest by the Romans in 254 BC. It was later one of the first bishoprics of the early Christian Church and in turn a stronghold of Gothic, Byzantine, Arab, Norman, Spanish and, in the eighteenth century, Bourbon rule. All these left marks of their culture, but Knight, searching only for the remains of Classical antiquity, overlooked all later periods and their remains and dismissed them as 'barbarous'.

44 Erice, the ancient Eryx, on Monte San Giuliano north-east of Trapani, is about eighty miles west of Monte Pellegrino near Palermo. Knight confuses Eryx with the ancient Heircte, a mountain near Palermo, which is sometimes identified with the modern Monte Pellegrino (see *Guida d'Italia del Touring Club Italiano*, XI (Milan 1953), 177–8). Hamilcar Barca (see n. 36) seized Mount Heircte in 247 BC and held the Romans at bay by frequent skirmishes. In 244 BC he advanced to Eryx, eighty miles west of Mount Heircte, but failed to relieve the siege of Drepana (Trapani). Knight's reading of the sources is obviously incorrect, and although he recognised Heircte from Polybius' description (see n. 45), he was looking for the remains of the 'wrong' camp.

45 Polybius (c.200–after 118 BC), Greek historian, described Rome's rise to world power in the forty books of his *Histories*. He describes Mount Heircte near Palermo (i.e. the modern Monte Pellegrino) in ed. Loeb (6 vols, London/New York 1922–7), I, 35 ff.

46 Today the Palazzo dei Normanni, formerly Palazzo Reale, begun by Roger II (AD 1130–54) and embellished by successive Norman kings.

47 The Cappella Palatina, built between 1132 and 1140 by Roger II (see n. 46), contains some of the finest surviving Byzantine mosaics. These were not appreciated by Knight or other eighteenth-century travellers, see H. Tuzet, op. cit. (n. 42 above), 282–3.

48 Sculptures of the third century BC, they once flanked the gateway of the Castello Maniace in Syracuse. One was destroyed during the revolution of 1848, the other is today in the National Archaeological Museum, Palermo, see P. Watkins, *See Sicily* (London 1974), 137.

49 Fazellus, op. cit. (n. 15 above), 96 BC.

50 Archbishop Francesco Testa of Monreale (until 1773), noted for his library and scientific interests, see *Johann Wolfgang Goethe. Gedenkausgabe der Werke, Briefe und Gespräche*, ed. E. Beutler (Zurich 1965), XIII, 1264, note on Monreale.

51 The Duomo (S. Maria la Nuova), founded by William I in 1174, acknowledged as one of the finest examples of Norman church architecture in Sicily, embellished with Byzantine mosaics of great beauty.

52 Died in 1166. The sarcophagus is still in the Duomo today.

53 Ancient site in north-west Sicily, one of the earliest settlements on the island. In the fifth century BC, the Segestans allied themselves with the Greeks to fight the Selinuntines, their traditional enemy. When this pact proved unsuccessful they sided with Carthage (410 BC). With the help of the Carthaginians, Selinunte was sacked in 409 BC, but as a result the Segestans came under the dominion of Carthage. In 307 BC Segesta was seized by Agathocles (361–289 BC), tyrant and king of Syracuse, who treated the population with exceptional barbarity, see T. J. Dunbadin, *The Western Greeks* (Oxford 1968), 326–9 and 336 ff.

In the First Punic War, Segesta immediately surrendered to the Romans and flourished until AD 25. For an introduction to the architecture and archaeology of this and other Doric sites in Sicily, see R. Koldewey and D. Puchstein, *Die griechischen Tempel in Unteritalien und Sizilien* (Berlin 1899). The temple at Segesta in particular is discussed by A. M. Burford in *Classical Quarterly* (London 1961), 87 ff. A watercolour of the site chosen by Knight to illustrate the diary is kept at the British Museum, Payne Knight Bequest (Oo.4-7; Pl. 3).

54 Cella = naos or inner chamber of a temple.

55 Entablature = in Classical architecture the arrangement of three horizontal bands (architrave, frieze and cornice) between capitals and pediment.

56 Virgil, *Aeneid*, V, 755–7: 'Meanwhile Aeneas traced the walls with a plough, and allotted dwellings: this he bade be Ilium, and these places Troy.'

57 Aeneas, a famous Trojan leader in Homer's *Iliad* and founder of Rome, is also the hero of Virgil's *Aeneid*. Aeneas had to overcome the hardships of long wanderings and loss of companions before he finally reached Italy. One of the stations of his journey was the country of the Elymi, where Acestes hospitably received him (*Aeneid*, V).

58 See n. 53 above.

59 Founded by Greek settlers c.650 BC on two eminences commanding a fertile plain, Selinus became the westernmost Greek colony in Sicily, in alliance with Carthage since 480 BC and in peaceful co-existence with Syracuse. In this period the Selinuntines were wealthy enough to build a series of temples but their long-standing enmity with Segesta (see n. 53) brought Athenian intervention in Sicily (415 BC). In 409 BC the Carthaginians invaded and Hannibal sacked Selinus. Refounded soon afterwards by refugees, it remained within Carthage's orbit until the Carthaginians destroyed it in 250 BC.

60 See n. 44 above.

61 For illustrations of the site selected by Knight, see British Museum, Payne Knight Bequest (Oo.4-10–22; Pls 4–6).

62 Herodotus (c.484–c.420 BC), Greek historian and traveller. His *History* is one of the main sources for ancient historiography. (Lot 755 in the *Sales Catalogue* is a 1715 edition of this work.) Herodotus mentions Selinus only once, ed. Loeb (4 vols, London/New York 1920–24), V, 46, and does not refer to the temple. Both Knight's references to Herodotus and Pausanias (see n. 63 below) must be based either on a vague memory or on other sources.

63 Pausanias of Lydia (?) (flourished c.AD 150), Greek traveller and geographer, wrote a *Description of Greece*. His only mention of Selinus concerns a treasury dedicated by the people of Selinus to Zeus at Olympia.

64 Abacus = the flat slab on the top of a capital. Triglyph = a three-grooved tablet forming part of a Doric frieze.

65 Intercolumnation = distance between two columns.

66 For an outline of Selinuntine history, see n. 59. The Carthaginians under Hannibal sacked the city in 409 BC but this is where Knight's accuracy ends.

Gisco was not (according to the *Oxford Classical Dictionary*) Hannibal's father but his nephew. Hannibal's father, according to Diodorus, whom Knight quotes on the history of Selinus (see n. 68), was in exile in Selinunte but not killed. His grandfather Hamilcar Barca (according to Diodorus' *History*, XIII, 59, 4–5; but according to the *Oxford Classical Dictionary* this was Hannibal's father) had been killed in a conflict with the Selinuntines, i.e. at the battle of Himera (see n. 36), but this is not likely to have been the reason for Hannibal's sacking of Selinus. All these events (apart from Gisco's role) are mentioned on the same page in Diodorus' account, which may be the reason why Knight refers to them together, if not in the correct sequence.

67 Strabo (see n. 9 above) does not mention the state of Selinus. Maybe Knight confuses him with Diodorus (see n. 85).

68 Diodorus Siculus (see n. 32 above), *History*, XIII, 57–9, describes the crimes committed after the taking of Selinus, but gives only a general account of the state of the buildings there (see n. 85).

69 Virgil, *Aeneid*, III, 705; 'I leave thee behind, palm-girt Selinus....'

70 *Pulce* = flea.

71 The ancient Acragas on the south-west coast of Sicily was founded c.582 BC by Greek colonists from Gela. The city prospered under successive tyrants, among them Phalaris (see n. 83) and Theron (see n. 36, 80). The latter conquered Himera in 476 BC and thereby resolved the intervention of the Carthaginians. He defeated them thoroughly in 480 BC with the aid of his brother-in-law Gelon, tyrant of Syracuse (see n. 93). After this victory Acragas undertook a grandiose building programme which included the huge Temple of the Olympian Zeus

(the Roman Jupiter) (see n. 76) and until the end of the fifth century enjoyed a long period of prosperity. Then, however, the Carthaginians renewed their attempt to conquer Sicily, captured Himera (see n. 36) and Syracuse and sacked Acragas in 406 BC after a long siege. It was rebuilt only after 338 BC by colonists from Syracuse, fell under Carthaginian dominion, was captured by the Romans in 261 BC and changed hands several times more before it finally became Roman in 210 BC.

The site occupies a large bowl of land which rises to an acropolis – with the temples of Hercules, Jupiter, Juno Lacinia, Concordia, Vulcan and Asclepius – on the north. The other side is protected by a ridge, and the whole site enclosed by a city wall, see G. Gruben, *Die Tempel der Griechen* (Munich 1966), 288–305.

Knight selected ten illustrations of the site: British Museum, Payne Knight Bequest (Oo.4-23–32).

72 The Temple of Juno Lacinia, today called Temple D (*c*.460–440 BC). Views of this temple by Hackert, Gore and Hearne are in the British Museum, Payne Knight Bequest (Oo.4-26, 30; Pls 7, 10).

73 The Temple of Concordia, today called Temple I (dedicated to the Dioskuroi?, *c*.450–440 BC). This temple owes its exceptional state of preservation to the fact that it was transformed into a Christian church in the sixth century AD. Views by Charles Gore are in the British Museum, Payne Knight Bequest (Oo.4-26, 30; Pls 7, 10).

74 Today called Temple A. A sepia drawing by Hackert is in the British Museum, Payne Knight Bequest (Oo.4-27; fig. 16).

75 Verres (see n. 30 above) hired thieves who in vain tried to lift the city's famous statue. They were surprised, stoned and driven away by the enraged Agrigentines, see Cicero, *The Verrine Orations*, II, IV, 43.

76 Diodorus (see n. 32 above), *History*, XIII, 82, 1–5. The Temple of Jupiter was begun after the victory at Himera (see n. 36) and left unfinished at the time of the Carthaginian destruction of the city in 406 BC. Its enormous scale puts it in the same class as the legendary temple of Diana at Ephesus. Illustrations of the building chosen by Knight are in the British Museum, Payne Knight Bequest (Oo.4-24 [frontispiece], 25).

77 Diodorus, *History*, XIII, 82, 2.

78 These sculptures are known only from the description by Diodorus (*History*, XIII, 82, 4).

79 Cicero, *The Verrine Orations*, II, IV, 43.

80 Hieron (died 467/6 BC) overthrew the tyranny of Acragas in 472 BC and succeeded his brother Gelon (see n. 93) as tyrant of Syracuse and Gela in 478. The building Knight refers to is, however, generally called the 'Tomb of Theron', who was tyrant of Acragas from 488 to 472 BC (see n. 71). It is situated in the area of the Roman necropolis between the temples of Concordia and Hercules, a typical Hellenistic *heroon* of Asia Minor form, dating from the first century BC, as Knight correctly deduced from its style. J. H. v. Riedesel, *Reise durch Sizilien und Grossgriechenland*, ed. G. Richter (Berlin 1965), 44–6, and P. Brydone, *A Tour through Sicily and Malta* (London 1773), I, 357, also comment on the monument.

81 Spirits of the dead in Roman mythology.

82 Philosopher and poet from Acragas (*c*.493–433 BC).

83 Neither of the two Hamilcars known to history (see n. 36) was involved in the destruction of Carthage in 406 BC. Knight presumably confuses it with the sacking of Himera.

Phalaris was tyrant of Acragas from *c*.570/65 to 554/49 BC. He became legendary for his ingenious cruelty, especially the hollow brazen bull in which his victims were roasted alive. Lot 456 in the *Sales Catalogue* is 'Bentley on the Epistles of Phalaris, 1777'.

84 Decimus Iunius Iuvenalis, Roman satiric poet, published his first extant satires between AD 100 and 110 and was still writing in AD 127. (An edition of 'Juvenalis et Persius, notis variorum, best edition, Amst. 1624' is in the *Sales Catalogue*, lot 503.)

The reference here is to Satire VIII, ed. Loeb, *Juvenal and Persius* (London/New York 1918), 105–11. The Loeb translation runs:

But after that come now a Dolabella, now an Antonius and now a sacrilegious Verres, loading big ships with secret spoils, peace-trophies more numerous than those of war.

Nowadays, on capturing a farm, you may rob our allies of a few yoke of oxen, or a few mares, with the sire of the herd; or of the household gods themselves, if there be a good statue left, or a single Deity in his little shrine.

85 Diodorus (see n. 32 above), *History*, XIII, 82, 1, describes the sacred buildings as buried or destroyed.

86 Daughter of Roger II, the first Norman king of Sicily (1130–54). She was married to Henry VI of Hohenstaufen, who crowned himself king of Sicily in 1194.

87 The sarcophagus of Phaedra was found near Agrigento in the eighteenth century. It is a Roman work of the second century AD. Knight recognised its Roman style, as is obvious from his comparison with the sarcophagus of Julia Mammaea.

Goethe (*Werke*, ed. E. Trunz [Munich 1978], XI, 273–4) and Riedesel (op. cit. [n. 80 above], 32–4) called the sarcophagus one of the finest examples of Greek (!) sculpture.

The carvings show scenes from the mythological tale of Phaedra and Hippolytus. On the front, Hippolytus, about to go on a hunt, learns of the love of his stepmother Phaedra. The other scenes show Phaedra's grief at her rejection by Hippolytus and Hippolytus' tragic death.

88 For a detailed discussion of Roman sarcophagi of this period see G. Koch and H. Sichterman, *Römische Sarkophage* (Munich 1982), 61–72.

89 Virgil, *Aeneid*, III, 703–4: 'Then steep Acragas, once the breeder of noble steeds, shows in the distance her mighty walls.'

90 Fazellus, op. cit. (n. 15 above), 133 C, 137 BCDE and 138 AB. Ph. Cluver's *Siciliae Antiquae* (Leiden 1723) appeared with Fazellus' work in the *Thesaurus* (see n. 15): on Gela 26 E, on Camarina 235 A–D.

91 Virgil, *Aeneid*, III, 700 ff.: '... *et fatis numquam concessa moveri/ apparet Camerina procul campique Geloi*' (... and afar off Camerina – Fate forbade that she ever be disturbed – is seen with the Geloan plains).

92 Pindar (518–438 BC), lyric poet born in Boeotia, went to Sicily in 476 BC where he worked for Hieron (see n. 80) and other Sicilian patrons. In his ode 'For Psaumis of Camarina', winner of the mule chariot race in 448 BC, *Olympian Odes*, ed. Loeb (London/New York 1915), V, 12, he wrote: 'Coming from the loved abodes of Oenomaüs and of Pelops, he singeth of thy holy precinct, O Pallas, thou guardian of the State, and the river Oânis, and the lake of the land, and the sacred streams with which Hipparis watereth the folk....'

93 First a Corinthian colony on the south-east coast of Sicily, founded in 734 BC, partly on the mainland (Achradina), partly on the connected small island of Ortygia, Syracuse became the centre of Greek power in Sicily for over 500 years. Its position was secured by natural defences: Ortygia as a salient protecting the two harbours, the long ridge of Epipolae forming a rampart against attacks from the hinterland and the marshes around the rivers Anapo and Ciane in the south. Many successful tyrants, among them Gelon (491–478 BC), Hieron I (see n. 80), Dionysius I (405–367 BC), Agathocles (317–289 BC) and Hieron II (265–215 BC), secured the city's position as the centre of Greek power and culture. Under the last of these it became an ally of Carthage, then fell to Rome in the Second Punic War and declined until Augustus sent a colony there in 21 BC.

94 A freshwater spring issuing from the tip of Ortygia. According to legend, the nymph Arethusa, pursued by the river-god Alpheus in the Peloponnese, leapt into the sea and was changed into a spring. To pursue her, Alpheus in turn changed into a river and his waters crossed the sea to Ortygia to mingle with those of Arethusa. The fountain provided a vital supply of fresh water during the many prolonged sieges the city had to endure.

95 Virgil, *Eclogues*, X, 4–5: 'If, when thou glidest beneath the Sicilian waves, thou wouldst not have briny Doris blend her stream with thine.'

96 Theocritus (*c*.300–260 BC), a native of Syracuse, composer of bucolic poems, hymns and short epics. Knight could here be referring to the poet's 'Idyll I', which describes the vain love of the nymph Daphnis for the shepherd Thyrsis. The scene is set in Sicily and at the foot of Mount Etna, though the fountain is not identified, see *Theocritus*, translation and commentary by A. S. F. Gow (Cambridge 1950), II, 1–32. For Virgil's description see n. 95.

97 *Basilissas philostidos* (Basilissa, daughter of Philostides); see n. 98.

98 The medal Knight mentions is reproduced and all its implications discussed by Jakob Philipp Orville in his *Sicula: quibus Siciliae veteris rudera illustrantur*, ed. P. Burmannus II (Amsterdam 1764), II, 460 and tav. XIV.

99 Notorious stone-quarries of Syracuse, used as prisons for a thousand Athenian soldiers captured after an unsuccessful siege of Syracuse in 413 BC, at which the Syracusans under Hieron I (see n. 80) destroyed an Athenian fleet in the Great Harbour (see n. 104).

100 Dionysius I (see n. 93) rebuilt the city's defences after the war with Athens, fought four wars against Carthage and even captured parts of eastern and southern Italy. His autocratic rule was unpopular in the more democratic parts of the Greek world, an attitude possibly reflected in Knight's description of his prisoners' sufferings. (P. Brydone, op. cit. [n. 80 above], I, 266–76, expresses similar sentiments in almost every respect.)

The 'Ear of Dionysius' is an artificially altered cave with a high pointed roof and an opening through which, according to the legend related by Knight, the tyrant used to eavesdrop on his prisoners.

101 Claudius Aelianus (*c*.AD 170–235), generally known as 'Aelian from Praeneste'. His extant works (*De Natura Animalum*, *Varia Historia*) deal with the idea of universal reason as manifested in the animal world. I have not been able to locate the particular reference to Philoxenus. (An edition of the *Varia Historia* is in the *Sales Catalogue*, lot 701.)

102 Philoxenus of Cythera (436/5–380/79 BC), poet at the court of Dionysius I (see n. 93), later sent to the Latomiae. His most famous work was *The Cyclops*, in which the cyclops sang a solo to the lyre.

103 Cicero, *The Verrine Orations*, II, v, 27. The Loeb edition quotes as follows:

Opus est ingens, magnificum regum ac tyrannorum; totum est e saxo in mirandam altitudinem depresso et multorum operis penitus exciso; nihil tam clausam ad exitum, nihil tam saeptum undique, nihil tam totum ad custodiam nec fieri nec cogitari potest

and translates:

... an immense and splendid piece of work carried out by the kings and tyrants. The whole thing is a profound excavation in the rock carried down to an astonishing depth by the labours of many stone-cutters; no prison more strongly barred, more completely enclosed, more severely guarded, could be constructed or imagined.

P. Brydone, op. cit. (n. 80 above), I, 270, uses exactly the same quotation to describe the caves.

104 The two remaining columns are depicted in a watercolour by Charles Gore, British Museum, Payne Knight Bequest (Oo.4-3; Pl. 12).

Athens, in an attempt to weaken Syracuse's growing influence in Magna Graecia, decided in the middle of her campaign against Sparta to carry the war to Sicily. In 415 BC the Athenians sent a fleet to Syracuse and landed their army on the shores of the Great Harbour. After the first battles they had to retreat across the Anapus (see n. 93). There followed a long siege until a relief force from Sparta succeeded in trapping the Athenian fleet after a final battle, and the surviving prisoners were sent to the Latomiae (see n. 99).

105 Marcus Claudius Marcellus, Roman general, in the Second Punic War commanded the blockade of Syracuse (213 BC) and took the city two years later, despite the engineering skills of Archimedes. See P. Brydone, op. cit. (n. 80 above), I, 281, for an account of his 'burning glasses'. When Marcellus entered the gates of Ortygia (opened from within), he is said to have been so amazed by the beauty and richness of the city that, although he plundered its treasures, he did not destroy the temples, palaces and other fine buildings.

106 For Dionysius see n. 93 and 100, for Hieron n. 80.

107 Cicero, *The Verrine Orations*, II, IV, 52.

108 Strabo (see n. 9 above), *Geography*, VI, 2, 6, mentions Selinus only briefly and does not even know whether it is inhabited in his time.

109 Formerly Catana, founded in 729 BC by Ionian Greeks, then ruled by tyrants in constant antagonism with Syracuse. (The people of Catana offered their city as a base for the Athenian attack on Syracuse, see n. 104.) It was destroyed by Dionysius I (see n. 93) after his victory over the Athenians. The city changed hands several times until the arrival of the Romans in 263 BC. Probably because of the few surviving ancient remains, Knight did not give an account of historical development of the city, as he had done for other places (see, for example, n. 36, 53, 59).

110 Vincenzo, Principe di Biscari (born 1742), the wealthiest and most learned man in Catania (see A. Momigliano, 'Ancient History and the Antiquarian', n. 10 above), was visited by all educated travellers who came to the city (see Tuzet, op. cit. [n. 42 above], 464–9).

114 Founded by Roger I, Count of Sicily, in 1092, it was destroyed by earthquake in 1169 and 1693. The building Knight saw had a contemporary façade, designed by the Sicilian architect G. B. Vaccarini in 1736. It incorporated granite columns recovered from the Roman theatre.

115 Sextus Pompeius Magnus Pius (*c*.67–36 BC), Roman general, son of Pompey.

116 In the Greek imagination Etna was variously the forge of Vulcan, the god of Fire, the forge of the Cyclops who inhabited this coast or the prison of the Titan Enceladus, who shook the earth in his efforts

to break free. However, already by the early seventeenth century, see Don Pietro Carvera, *Descriptio Aetna* (1623) and *Il Mongibello* (1636), the volcano had also become a matter of scientific interest. Sir William Hamilton, English Ambassador at Naples, antiquarian, connoisseur and colleague of Knight's (see *Arrogant Connoisseur*, 50 ff.) had described geological phenomena on the mountain several years earlier, see W. Hamilton, *Voyage au Mont Etna*, translated from the English by Villebois and published as an appendix to Riedesel's account, op. cit. (n. 80 above) in 1773. Hamilton published it in English in his *Campi Phlegraei* (Naples 1776), which was widely read among travellers and collectors. Knight, who knew Hamilton well, seems to owe a great deal to his observations, as well as those of Brydone, op. cit. (n. 80 above), I, 104–262, and Riedesel, op. cit., 125 ff.

117 Knight is obviously referring to Riedesel's account, op. cit. (n. 80 above), 125, which he must have read, if not before his journey, certainly before he wrote the final version of the diary.

118 The ascent to the crater followed a certain route including fixed resting places, one of which was the 'Grotta del Capro'. Thomas Fazellus (see n. 15) had already climbed the same way in the sixteenth century (see H. Tuzet, op. cit. [n. 42 above], 243).

J. R. Cozens' poetic interpretation of this cave after a sketch by Charles Gore (for details see C. F. Bell and T. Girtin, *Walpole Society* XXIII [London 1934–5], II, and *Arrogant Connoisseur*, 29–30) is in the British Museum, Payne Knight Bequest (Oo.4-38; Pl. 14).

119 Tasso, *La Gerusalemme Liberata*, ed. U. Hoepli (Milan 1912), Canto XIV, 10. Hoole's translation of 1792 runs:

Survey yon sea, the mighty and the vast!
Which here can no such glorious title claim
A pool unnoted and a worthless name.

120 The pillar, rod, etc. which indicates the time of day on a sundial.

121 For an account of the Canon's character and discoveries, see H. Tuzet, op. cit. (n. 42 above), 486–91, and n. 137 below.

122 Milton, *Paradise Lost*, I, 80 (*Complete Poetry and Selected Prose*, ed. E. H. Visiak [Glasgow 1964]):

O how unlike the place from whence they fell!
There the companions of his fall o'erwhelmed
With Floods and Whirlwinds of Tempestuous Fire
He soon discerns . . .

123 Charles Gore gives a complete (and very similar) account of the party's ascent to the crater on the verso of his watercolour sketches relating to the event. They are preserved in the Goethe-Nationalmuseum, Weimar (Th. Scr. 2.2³ ff.).

124 A massive, largely Roman construction, the original of which is said to have been built in the time of Hieron II, the last tyrant of Syracuse. The irresistible 'postcard' view of Mount Etna through the collapsed scena of the theatre has attracted numerous visitors – among them Goethe – to Taormina.

125 Greek philosopher and poet of the fifth century BC.

126 The so-called *naumachia* is a brick wall below the forum of the city which, in fact, formed the outer wall of a larger two-aisled cistern.

127 Anciently Zancle, a Greek colony on the Straits of Messina in north-west Sicily, founded *c.*730 BC. With its desirable position, guarded to the rear by mountains and with a superb natural harbour commanding the strait through which the Mediterranean trade was channelled, Zancle prospered. It was soon contested by Athens and Syracuse and later by the Carthaginians, who in 306 BC destroyed the city. In the First Punic War it formed an alliance with Rome and became the Romans' most important naval base in the Mediterranean. The inde-

pendent spirit which characterised Messina in ancient times prevailed again in her resistance to the cruelty of the Angevins (1282) and the rebellion against the neglectful viceroys of Spain in the seventeenth century. An extraordinary series of catastrophes – epidemics of the plague and cholera, earthquakes, etc. – destroyed the city in that period.

128 Faro = the Straits of Messina.

129 Norman period (1061–1194), Swabian period (1194–1268) and Aragonese period (1282–1410).

130 Count Roger, later Roger I, and Robert de Hauteville seized Messina in 1061 at the head of a small band of Norman knights. In a series of campaigns lasting thirty years they gradually won Sicily from the Saracens.

131 Spanish period (1410–1713). Messina had in 1535 welcomed Charles V of Spain as her protector. However, by the mid-seventeenth century the Spanish rulers were detested and during the course of a rebellion in 1674, Messina sought the aid of Louis XIV, King of France, who sent a fleet under the command of Duquesne. In 1678, however, he decided to abandon the Messinians. The Spanish rulers punished the city by stripping it of all privileges. The population was reduced from 120,000 to 15,000. Messina recovered in the early eighteenth century but was hit by natural catastrophes. The city was almost completely destroyed by an earthquake in 1783, see *Guida d'Italia del Touring Club Italiano*, XI (Milan 1953), 400.

132 See n. 131 above.

133 Lot 578 in the *Sales Catalogue* is: 'Davila, Guerre Civile da Francia. Ven. 1642'.

134 In Homer's *Odyssey*, ed. Loeb (2 vols, London/New York 1919), XII, 101 ff., a sort of whirlpool or maelstrom in a narrow channel of the sea, later identified with the Straits of Messina. In poetry and legend the whirlpool was personified as a female monster which sucked in and cast out the water three times a day and destroyed every ship trying to pass through the Straits.

135 Virgil, *Aeneid*, III, 420–23. 'Charybdis, insatiate, [guards] the left; and at the bottom of her seething chasm thrice she sucks the vast waves into the abyss, and again in turn casts them upwards, lashing the stars with spray.'

136 The return journey – via Naples – is recorded in an illustration by Thomas Hearne, British Museum, Payne Knight Bequest (Oo.4-4). It is inscribed 'View of Monte Cassino. on the Road from Naples, July 1777', Monte Cassino being a Benedictine Abbey between Rome and Naples.

137 The British traveller in question was Patrick Brydone, who in his work on Sicily, op. cit. (n. 80 above), I, 131–2, had reported how Recupero had made detailed studies of the geology of Mount Etna. The Canon had found various layers of lava and from their structure had concluded that each would have taken two thousand years to form. This meant that the oldest had to be more than 14,000 years old. These scientific results clashed with the latest exegetical researches – Mount Etna would have existed before the creation of the world – and the bishop intervened. (The controversy is discussed in greater detail in H. Tuzet, op. cit. [n. 42 above], 486–92.)

138 Victor Amédée II (1666–1732), Duke of Savoy, became King of Sicily and Sardinia in 1713.

139 Frederick II of Hohenstaufen, crowned Frederick I of Sicily in 1197. Knight may, however, be referring to Roger II, the first Norman King of Sicily (1130–54), who drew up the earliest code of law.

140 Knight must here be referring to Patrick Brydone's work, op. cit. (n. 80 above), I, 67 ff., which devoted a whole chapter to the 'Bandits of Sicily', and described them in literally the same terms. Brydone's account of the Sicilian climate (ibid., II, 63 ff. and 138 ff.) is very close to Knight's too. Why Knight gives his initials as HVB is difficult to understand.

141 Similar notions appear in the works of Voltaire and d'Alembert who, despite differences in other matters, agree that in historical texts one is informed only about the 'history of the vultures', while the endeavours of human intellect are rarely described: see R. Eisler, *Historisches Wörterbuch der Philosophie*, rev. ed. J. Ritter (Darmstadt 1961–), II, 'Geschichte'.

142 Horace, *Epistles*, ed. Loeb (London/New York 1926), II, II, 176. I am grateful to Brian Cook for the source of this quotation.

143 Knight had used the juxtaposition between luxury and refinement on one hand and the hardy, warlike attitudes necessary for survival in less secure circumstances on the other, to explain the fall of Acragas and Syracuse. This reflects ideas put forward in Montesquieu's work (see n. 145), with which Knight was familiar.

144 'If you would be loved, be lovable.' Ovid, *The Art of Love*, ed. Loeb (London/New York 1929), II, 107.

145 Knight's ideas on education, especially of women, are progressive. He may well have been influenced by the popular works on the issue by F. Salignac de la Mothe Fénelon and John Locke; for details, see Eisler, op. cit. (n. 141 above), I, 'Aufklärung'.

146 Charles de Secondat, Baron de la Brède et de Montesquieu (1689–1755), philosophical historian, deals at great length with the effect of climate on the national character in his *L'Esprit des Lois* (1748–50), chapters XIV–XVII.

147 The idea that the history of Sicily had to be seen as a series of revolutions had been put forward by the two major historians of the island in the early eighteenth century: G. B. Caruso, in his *Memorie istoriche di quanto è accaduto in Sicilia dal tempo dei suoi primieri abitatori sino alla coronazione del re Vittorio Amadeo* (1716) and I. Levesque de Burigny in his *Histoire générale de Sicile* (1745).